If you are an Aussie man, read this book. If you are a man anywhere, read this book. If you are a man, Aussie or otherwise, who wants to grow your business rapidly, sell a shedload of whatever it is you make, and make massive revenues and profits accordingly, read this book. Bec Brideson's given you all the information you need. Get over the belief that you have nothing to learn from women, or nothing to learn about women, and buy and read this book. Bec writes, 'Why is it that when we see the word "gender" in the context of "business" our insides feel tight and we run for the hills?' Don't be a business coward — be a future forward business genius. Exploit the hell out of this book to own the future and make an absolute goddamn fucking shit-ton of money — because there is a huge amount of money to be made out of taking women seriously.

Cindy Gallop, Former Chairman of Bartle Bogle Hegarty, Founder of MakeLoveNotPorn and IfWeRanTheWorld

Bec Brideson is a smart, effective and powerful person so of course she would write a smart, effective and powerful book.

Jane Caro, novelist, author, social commentator

As women grow their influence — at home, in the workplace and in the world — it exponentially opens up new opportunities for businesses who are able to connect with women in a meaningful and authentic way. Packed full of cutting edge insights, facts and practical advice, Blind Spots is an indispensable resource for anyone who wants to get ahead of the game in an increasingly accelerated and female empowered world.

Margie Warrell, ambassador for *Women in Global Business* and bestselling author of *Stop Playing Safe* and *Make Your Mark*

T0323969

Blind Spots, is essential reading for anyone who is serious about growing their business in the twenty-first century. All the hard work has been done for you. The critical academic research distilled, the evidence explained and the key insights presented in a manner which can be easily digested and acted upon immediately. Literally, everything you need to know about engaging women and opening their purses, is contained within this remarkable book.

Michael Faudet, former creative director, DDB

Bec has written a book that urges business 'to get women and get rich.' If you only read one business book this year, make it this one. Her thinking is original, her instructions are practical and her life experience both as a woman and as a marketing professional make her insights compelling. She asks, 'Why don't marketers see women for what they are? They are the world's greatest unrealised business opportunity. They are the largest untapped target market, with the greatest power to spend. It's not just baffling, it's bad business.'

Rod Bennett, founder, BADJAR Group

BLIND SPOTS

BLIND
SPOTS

HOW TO UNCOVER & ATTRACT THE FASTEST EMERGING ECONOMY

RJ BRIDESON

WILEY

First published in 2018 by John Wiley & Sons Australia, Ltd

42 McDougall St, Milton Qld 4064

Office also in Melbourne

Typeset in 11/16pt Helvetica Neue LT Std

The moral rights of the author have been asserted

National Library of Australia Cataloguing-in-Publication data:

Creator:	Brideson, Bec, author.
Title:	Blind Spots : how to uncover and attract the fastest emerging economy / Bec Brideson.
ISBN:	9780730345404 (pbk.)
	9780730345381 (ebook)
Notes:	Includes index.
Subjects:	Women consumers — Influence.
	Women — Economic aspects.
	Target marketing.
	Consumer behavior.
	Purchasing power — Comparative method.

Cover design by Wiley

Internal design by Kiriaki Sarafis

Printed in Singapore by C.O.S. Printers Pte Ltd

10 9 8 7 6 5 4 3 2 1

Disclaimer

The material in this publication is of the nature of general comment only, and does not represent professional advice. It is not intended to provide specific guidance for particular circumstances and it should not be relied on as the basis for any decision to take action or not take action on any matter which it covers. Readers should obtain professional advice where appropriate, before making any such decision. To the maximum extent permitted by law, the author and publisher disclaim all responsibility and liability to any person, arising directly or indirectly from any person taking or not taking action based on the information in this publication.

CONTENTS

FOREWORD

Never in history has there been more pressure on businesses. The average time a CEO keeps their job is near record lows. The average time a marketing director keeps theirs is even shorter — just 44 months.

It's not hard to see why.

We've moved from a business environment where successful companies could hold the same steady course for decades to a corporate battlefield that is being ripped apart by the ubiquitous forces of the internet — instant global markets and competition, extreme transparency and competitiveness on pricing, and the rise of the consumer's voice via social media, blogs and product reviews.

And it isn't about to slow down anytime soon.

One of the most important consequences of these seismic shifts in the marketplace is that the basic, bland and shallow manner in which so many companies have traditionally communicated with their potential customers is no longer working.

These days what companies say in their marketing messages and what they do day-to-day in the world are revealed, commented upon and evaluated within hours by their customers. Speak down to them and your company will be discussed and derided globally almost instantly. Be trite, simplistic or just inaccurate in how you communicate with them, and they'll abandon your brand for the ten thousand others on the internet that offer pretty much the same things you do.

As the mass media devolves into the mess media, we have never been more in need of a new breed of communication expert who can help us navigate our way through the message minefield.

At the forefront of these pundits is Bec Brideson, a genuine expert on one of the most important areas of commerce — the female customer.

Just as the Inuit are said to have 50-plus words to describe different types of snow, where we see only one, Bec Brideson can identify a myriad ways we can better communicate with women, many of which the average senior executive has never even thought about, let alone addressed.

Bec doesn't just understand women. She has articulated a precise path for how businesses can see them, resonate with them, communicate with them and then do business with them.

This priceless knowledge was not acquired easily. It has taken Bec more than 25 years of focused work in the communications industry — first as a multi-award winning advertising writer, then as a top-level creative director, then running her own agency specialising in marketing to women, and now as a nationally respected consultant advising companies on her cutting-edge methodology for reaching (and persuading) the female consumer.

Knowledge is one thing, but what makes Bec so valuable to businesses is her commercial acumen. She understands that companies aren't marketing for kicks, but for bucks. And that's why this book is packed with insights that can help you sell truckloads of products and services to the female customer.

Some of what she says may shock you, much of it will challenge you, but by the end you'll agree on two things:

There's a much more effective way to communicate and sell to the female consumer.

Bec Brideson knows exactly how to do it.

Siimon Reynolds
bestselling author of
Why People Fail
April 2017

ABOUT THE AUTHOR

R. J. (Bec) Brideson has a mission to change the world's attitudes to women, economics and business.

A pioneer and innovator in commercially smart ways to market to the female consumer, she helps organisations develop strategies and solutions to make more money in what is the fastest growing economic market.

With over twenty years of success as a communications specialist, Bec is recognised for her work on big brands across categories such as FMCG, automotive and aviation, including the successful launch of Virgin Airlines in Australia. She is one of only 3 per cent of women globally to have held the job title of Creative Director, and is renowned for setting up Australia's first marketing-to-women agency, Venus Comms.

Now an influential facilitator, trainer, mentor and coach, Bec helps business leaders and organisations to uncover what women really want, expect and need from them and to transform this understanding into business growth.

She believes that a company's true competitive advantage is way more obvious and accessible than many think. From C-suite to CMOs, executive teams, digital, marketing and sales departments, Bec has proved time and time again the financial upside of womenomics.

Her ability to create clarity and focus around an industry and topic that is often misheard and misunderstood makes her a sought-after speaker. She has presented at numerous conferences throughout the world, including Cannes Lions, Indi Summit, Pause Fest, ad:tech and Mumbrella360.

Bec is married to an 'adman' and has two young daughters. This is her first (but definitely not her last) book.

ACKNOWLEDGEMENTS

For just over a year, I set my alarm for 4.45 am so I could focus on my writing in a still and quiet house. It has taken me daily discipline and commitment to bring this book to its full potential, which is exactly how I propose you improve your own business.

I feel my purpose is to create a better world for womankind, mankind and human kindness. We all have an opportunity to add richness, warmth and value, and to help lighten the load for others. This book, I hope, is a step in this direction.

It takes a village to raise a child, and a community to write a book.

To my community:

Kelly Irving, my patient, clever and supportive editor, to whom I'm profoundly grateful. Lucy Raymond at Wiley — I am in awe of your strength and courage. Melissa Kuttan, my intelligent business assistant and cheer squad, and all of the Venus team, particularly Kiki Sarafis for brilliant design aesthetics and Sive Buckley, who 'calms my farm'. Looking back on my career: Sean Cummins for the craft and the guts, and for being the catalyst to my steely determination and belief. Michael Faudet and Rod Bennett, two of the cleverest creative men in advertising, who believed in me at various stages along my career path and who championed me on my journey both in and out of the ad industry.

To my village:

My loving parents for the DNA, the opportunity and the education you gave your daughters. My sister Meg, my bestie Angie Douglas, my clever cousin Melanie Sheppard, and other women in my tribe including Georgia Murch, Jayne Ansin, Bec Cole, Donna McCrum, Tara Lordsmith and Chris Khor. You are all wonderful and strong women who lift me up and embolden me.

And to my husband, who had the courage to join me in life before joining me in my business. For the intellectual rigour, the productive debates, the development of our knowledge and the tough times we survived juggling babies and business and getting through it all. To my girls, Miffy and Winsome: thank you for being the strong, resilient and creative darlings you are. There is no end to my appreciation of my family for supporting me in my career and passion outside of the other most important job in the world — loving you all.

PREFACE

Imagine a page with the heading '**Gender**' at the top. On one side we list issues that we encounter in the **HR** or **culture department**, such as unconscious bias, wage gap, glass ceiling, equal opportunity and workforce diversity.

Somewhere at the bottom of the page we note more personal subjects around **sexuality and identity**, such as transgender evolutions, sexual preferences and the blurring of domestic roles.

Then over on the other side of the page we add another large heading, '**Womenomics**' or '**The female economy**', then note down some of the economic issues relating to women's impact in the marketplace and their financial leverage today in the consumer economy.

Now many of these points can be connected by dotted or blurry lines, but still they are all very different subjects.

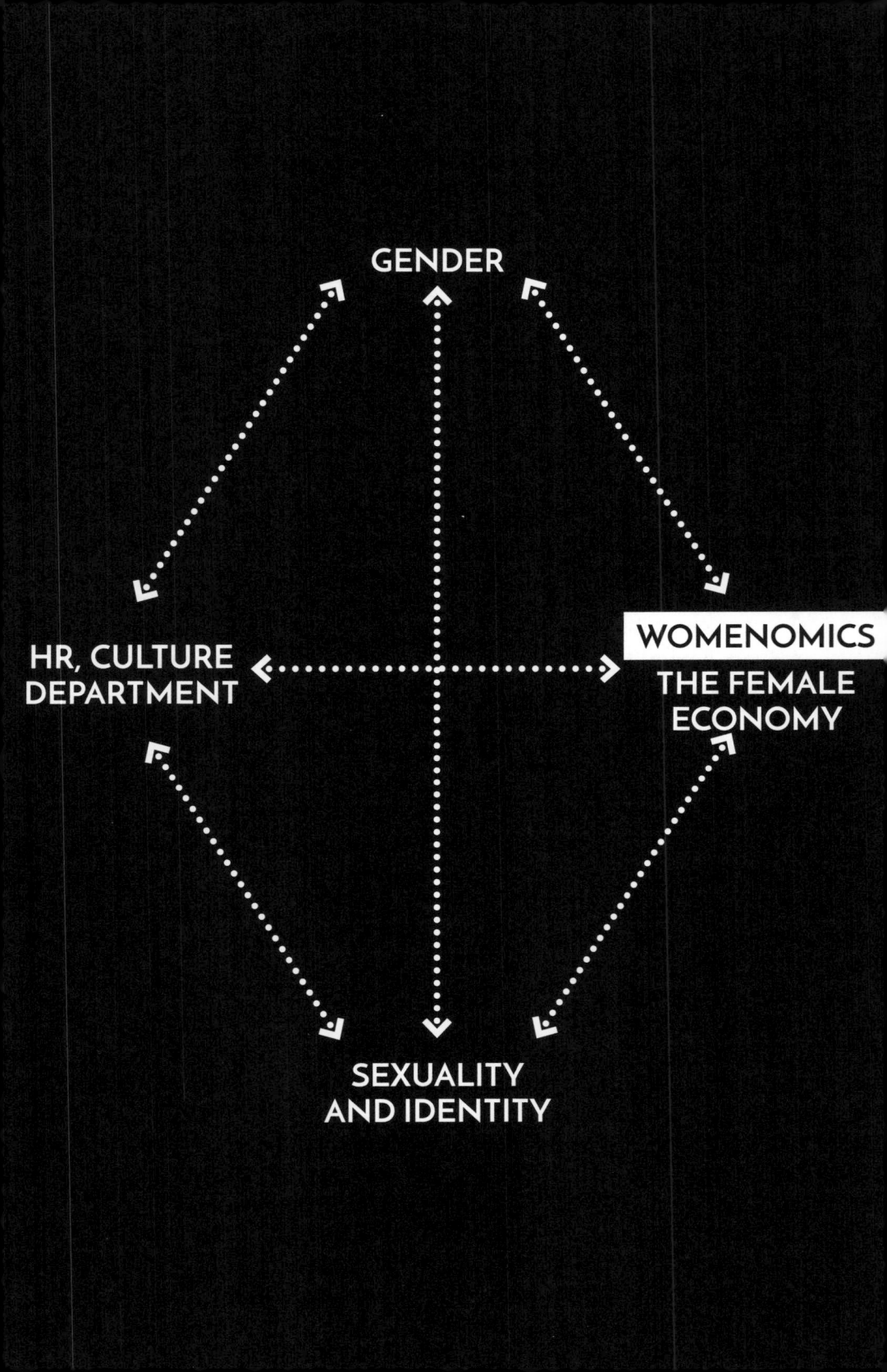

GENDER

HR, CULTURE
DEPARTMENT

WOMENOMICS
THE FEMALE
ECONOMY

SEXUALITY
AND IDENTITY

It is no wonder that confronting these issues is inherently confusing, which often means this useful exercise ends up in the 'too hard basket'.

On the HR side, many workplace headaches and difficulties can make us feel a bit uneasy, emotional or just worn out. Years of discussion of all this have made us a bit weary and wary, but treating genders equally while celebrating their differences is such an important dynamic when it comes to moving society forward. Unconscious bias is tricky because normally it is not visible on the surface. So if it is not apparent, how do we tackle it?

Sexuality and gender roles are so much wrapped up in personal preferences and lifestyle values that it's a bit like our political inclinations: we don't usually go around discussing them or justifying them because they involve individual choice. Nonetheless these issues often crop up at work and need to be understood because of the way they can affect the business or financial discussions of males and females as markets.

That women have a distinctive economic role is a fairly new revelation in the business world. Many business leaders don't know about it or understand it, or they don't see it as relevant to their bottom line. For many different reasons, they think the homogenising of gender is not an issue. They have traditionally viewed the world through a male lens, and they don't see why we should upset the applecart by changing this now.

'Gender' is a word that makes many of us shrink and feel instantly defensive. It speaks to who we are in everyday life: the way we dress, which bathroom we use, how we identify ourselves and others. That's why it's a subject of nuance, and often confusion, and a political hot potato. But that doesn't mean we should ignore it.*

*I'm going to show you why
we need to think otherwise.

or a woman, presenting these arguments is especially problematic, or a really simple reason: most people think they are about to enter nto an 'HR / bias / feminist' discussion. Not true!

As a woman working in this market, I have built something of a reputation as an expert on gender opportunity. Still I find that many would rather dismiss such concerns as 'women's problems' than take the time to understand that I am talking about ways the business might be more financially successful.

Culture/workplace gender issues, sexuality, the female economy (womenomics). When writing this book, I worked to keep the three subjects distinct in order to better understand them and appreciate what each brings to the discussion. But the fact is they are all part of the overall mix, so keep that page in your head and continue to visualise those dotted lines linking them. As you read this book, I hope you will start to see gender as a wonderfully powerful term associated with profits, product developments and market disruption, rather than as big blind spots.

The numbers and facts around womenomics are black and white, but there is still a big grey area to address — and that's what we'll be doing in the pages that follow.

$

Addressing our gender differences, when it comes to business, can lead to big bucks — so stick with me!

This book was written for forward-thinking trailblazers who are ready to take positive action in their businesses and organisations. It closes the gap between wanting to create change and knowing why we need it. It's for those decision makers who are having the conversation but are struggling with how to look at it all from a new perspective. And it's for the leaders at the top who will be influenced by the determined, enterprising folk who work with them.

Together, we'll bridge all levels of the organisational chart to explore how acknowledging our different perspectives can add up to more revenue.

We'll look at how tradition has created a false myopia and why learning to see the way the world has changed can illuminate some of the blind spots that persist in corporations around the globe today. To *not* see gender is to limit yourself to one perspective or lens and to miss the greater opportunity entirely. If you will suspend your disbelief and keep both your eyes and your mind wide open, this book will be transformational to your future business.

Let's begin.

....INTRODUCTION

Women are the fastest growing global consumer economy.

An Ernst and Young study reports that by 2028 women will control close to 75 per cent of discretionary spend worldwide.[1] That's a trillion-dollar opportunity for the business world — a world that has been shaped by men and an instinctive male perspective.

Is it any wonder
that big blind spots
exist in businesses and
brands when it comes
to forming relationships
with women?

Put simply, you are failing to seize a trillion-dollar business opportunity because you have no idea how to address this paradox by looking at your business from a different perspective.

If you're like most CEOs, then you're looking to technology, innovation and 'disruption' for competitive advantage, but I suggest you're getting it all wrong! The solution is devastatingly simple and right in front of you.

You are viewing the consumer world through only one lens. A traditional, male lens. Now it's time to include a female lens.

Many leading business execs say they already have a healthy bottom line. So why would they change their current formula if it's working well?

Why consider ways to better meet the unmet needs or wants of women *and make more money by doing so?*

The answer is really as simple as:

'Why wouldn't you?'

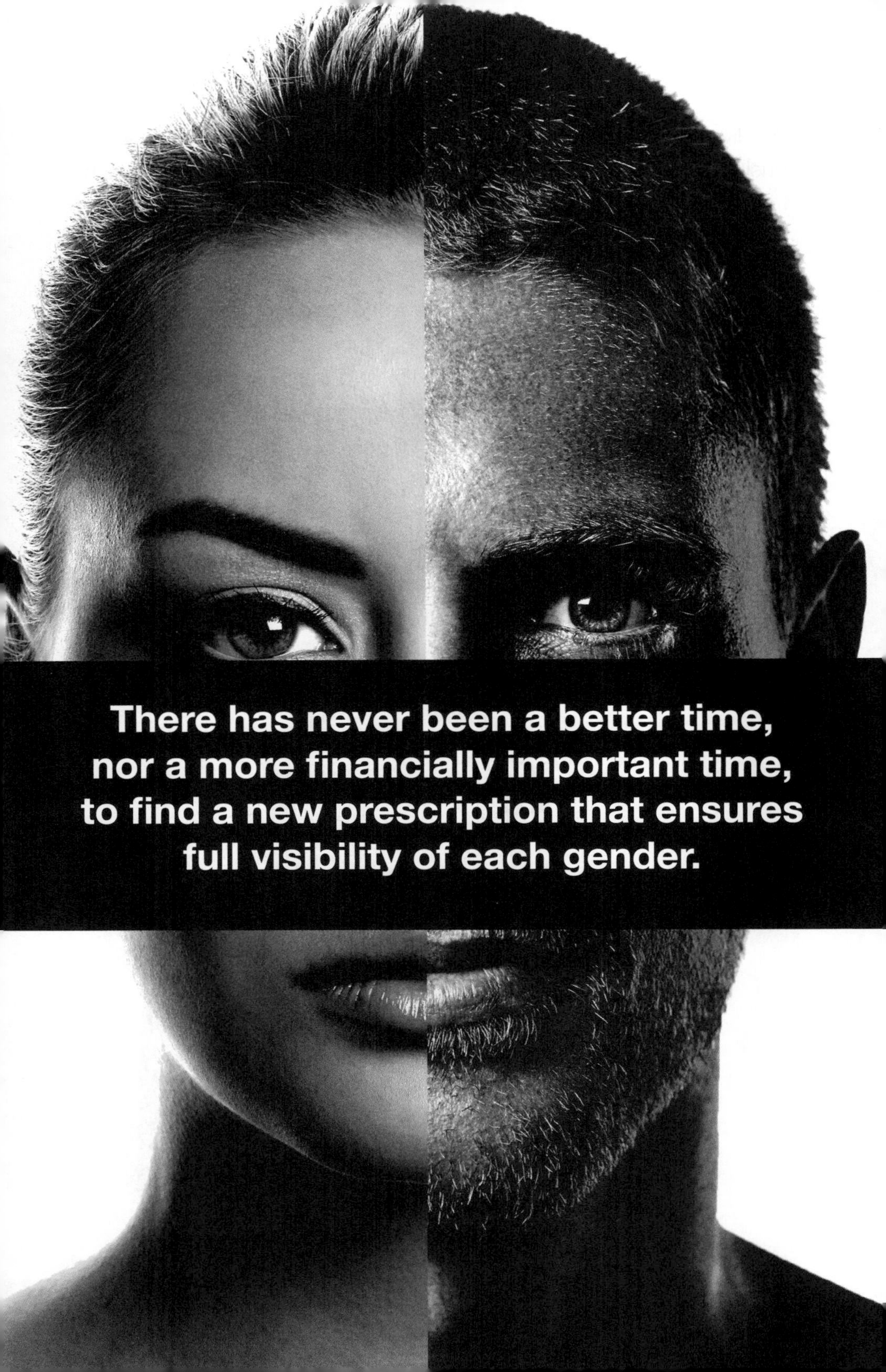

There has never been a better time,
nor a more financially important time,
to find a new prescription that ensures
full visibility of each gender.

We live in a time of exponential change and disruption. Being a business that thrives in today's landscape requires a new approach. Leaders must learn about, understand and harness the ever-changing competitive market.

Three unrelenting forces shaping the world today are the weather, the web and women. At the same time, education and entrepreneurial opportunities are increasingly 'fast, flat and free'. The democratising internet has broken down barriers for women, encouraging them to make their own way onto the world stage.

Women use the web to start up their businesses, connect to one another, buy and sell, communicate their delight and dissatisfaction. Women also research businesses and spend money with them like never before, aligning with brands that share their values.

WOMEN HOLD
THE POWER
TO PROFIT.

The web has given women a platform from which they can be heard 24 hours a day, 7 days a week. They are building community and recognition, relevance and legitimacy in a space that is no longer monopolised by the traditionally dominant traditional-lensed perspective. Women own one-third of all businesses, more than half of which are in developing countries.[2]

Lots of smart people out there nod knowingly, eyes widening as they lean in to hear more. You progressive forward thinkers recognise that you need to improve now to set yourself up for the future.

The naysayers who dismiss the opportunities risk finding themselves sidelined, classified with companies that have famously failed to recognise and embrace earlier critical transitions — from steam to electric trains, from celluloid film to digital, from print to online communication.

It's likely you employ women, probably in your marketing team, which means you already understand the female market, right?

Wrong.

Your female employees, staff, team, colleagues, clients and customers have spent a lifetime learning from a rulebook that was invented and passed down with that traditional male lens. But we live in a new era.

This is fact. It's not man bashing. It's not personal.

It's just better business.

Whether you're a woman or a man, it's not your fault that you've been applying or acceding to an unconscious bias.

For both women and men, this is an exciting opportunity — an invitation — to re-examine the business world from a female-lensed perspective.

We're at the beginning of a market renaissance — a woman's revolution. It's an economic boom that could make or break your business and brand.

To embrace this opportunity, to get it right, you must have a clear understanding of the role of gender in your market. Or, to put it bluntly, you've got to stop seeing everything through the traditional male lens and learn how to also include a female lens!

This is what this book will show you how to do.

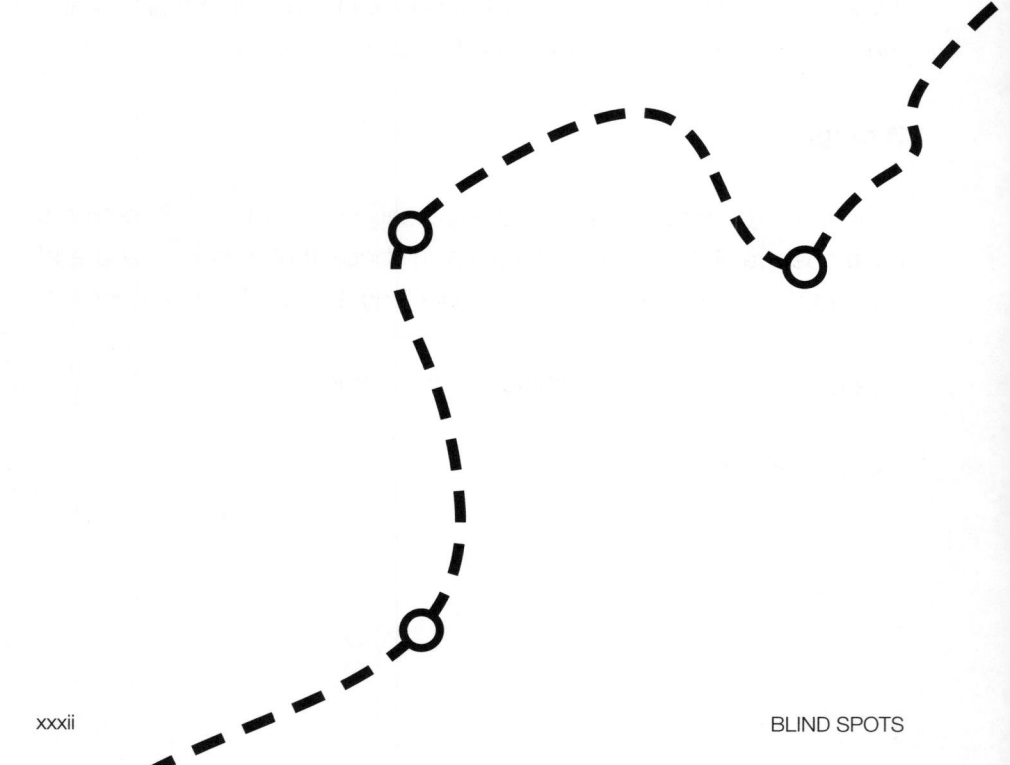

WE'LL EXPLORE:

- how we arrived at this point in business and the lessons we need to learn to adapt to a future, forward-thinking market

- what brands have it right and what brands have it all wrong

- how the sexes really think, operate and therefore shop (hint: it has nothing to do with the colour pink)

- why having a female workforce is a great start, but not the only thing you have to do

- how to better see and engage with female consumers

- how to communicate your business and brand to boost your bottom line and benefit everyone, male and female.

A WO-MANIFESTO

Sure, it's bold and audacious to suggest that there's a new female-focused way forward. But, as you'll soon see, this book is full of bold and audacious perspectives.

I know what works and doesn't work when it comes to women. Not just because I'm a woman, but because I've worked in the communications business for over 25 years and have seen it with my own eyes. From business culture to research, product development to communication, I understand how great the opportunity is to better cater to unmet female needs, wants and wallets.

In 2004, I opened Australia's first advertising agency to specialise in marketing to women. Through Venus Comms I've developed proven methodologies that create a whole new perspective on the lucrative and dominating market force that is women, all of which I will share with you in this book. As a mentor and coach, I've worked with businesses large and small, leading executives and CEOs (both male and female) in most industries from retail to sport, fashion to finance.

We can all collectively benefit from adjusting the current paradigms of business based on historical ways of building successful empires. The data, tried and tested strategies, stories, examples and case studies that follow will demonstrate why the time is now and how you too can use this power. This is a shared opportunity for all who believe in the power of transformation to meet your market needs.

Decades ago, no-one imagined a future dominated by smartphones, online commerce and artificial intelligence, despite the early signs. We are now living in a new world and a new economy.

It's time to get businesses and marketing right when it comes to women, and their many unmet needs.

It's time to get down to business.

It's time to recognise the blind spots.

Are you ready to change the way you've been viewing your world?

GRAB 'EM BY THE 'PURSE-Y'

This book explores the current and future costs and impacts on organisations that fail to meet the needs of the world's fastest growing market — women. Here's what's at stake.

1. Female spending power is at an unprecedented high — projected to be an up to $28 trillion opportunity.[3]

2. She is the chief purchasing officer in the home, making nine out of ten household decisions.[4]

3. She accumulates more assets and controls more private wealth than an high-stock company.[5]

4. More and more female entrepreneurs and business owners are on the rise and in control.[6]

5. Women will control 75 per cent of global discretionary spend within the next ten years.[7]

6. Over the next five years, working women will drive an estimated $6 trillion increase in earned income globally.[8]

CHAPTER 1

FROM
HISTORY
TO
HERSTORY

Eve was quietly minding her own business, admiring all the delights that Paradise was delivering. How might she use some of the amazing garlands and tendrils to decorate her own backyard? She contemplated asking Adam for help. Perhaps they could make it a joint home improvement project. Or would she need to outsource the task?

Suddenly, out of nowhere, the Serpent rose up at her feet, invading her personal space, and proceeded to tempt Eve with a free trial of an apple.

Sceptical though she was of the Serpent's crude sales pitch and evident inability to read her uncomfortable body language and grimacing facial cues, she agreed mainly in the hope he'd quickly slither away.

Still resentful of his opportunism, she tentatively took a bite.

And surprisingly it wasn't at all bad. In fact, Eve was delighted with how the product delivered on taste and crunch, so she took another bite of the mouth-watering fruit.

She hesitated on the third bite. How many calories did this contain? Was it on her approved dietary checklist? Would it ruin her dinner plans? But having accepted the free sample she felt obliged to test it properly, so soon she was justifying her behaviour with the adage 'an apple a day keeps the doctor away'.

It wasn't long, though, before the dissonance she felt set off an inner dialogue concerning her decision making, and she started analysing why she had accepted the Serpent's product.

What example would she be setting for future females?

She was annoyed with herself that she'd let him talk her into something she wasn't actually interested in, although her non-verbal cues should have told him this. But she felt disappointed that she hadn't just spoken up and said 'no means no' and seen her wishes respected.

By her fifth bite she'd made sense of her 'post-purchase dissonance' and added a definitive black mark against the 'Serpent Apple' brand. That sales guy really needed to think about customer interaction, specifically when, how and where women should be approached. That kind of 'prey and spray' ambush move was not going to cut it in the long term.

And so history was made in the Garden of Eden.

Here was the first recorded act of marketing, and it targeted a female consumer. Sure, it's only a story, but whether it's true or not doesn't change the fact that to this day females are a major target when we market our products. And that we target women as though they were men.

Today women are responsible for up to nine out of ten consumer spending decisions, and influence 80 to 85 per cent of household spending.[1]

THE BIRTH OF BUSINESS MARKETING

Marketing as we know it was first framed by our business forefathers. It was conceived 150 years ago as both an academic discipline and a business practice based on success and survival through domination — in other words, an intrinsically male perspective.

From its beginnings around 1870, marketing reflected the production principle of demand exceeding supply. Business focused on building things — stock and product — rather than on customers.[2] By the turn of the century unprecedented growth and innovation meant supply had caught up with demand.

As business boomed in the early decades of the twentieth century, competition increased and marketing became the practice of pushing products onto consumers through sales. Thus, marketing's definition broadened to analysis of the consumer's wants and needs and how to connect product and customer.

Through the 1940s to the 1960s, the supply still exceeded demand and marketing's focus became putting the consumer at the centre of

the business and delivering what consumers wanted.[3] It's important to note, though, that little gender distinction was made, which in effect meant a default to a traditional masculine perspective, because throughout these decades very few women had broken out of the domestic sphere and into professional or academic roles.[4] Marketing and business was therefore a male-lensed exercise, even if the products being made and sold were for women.

It also makes sense that during the first half of the twentieth century the language of business strategy and marketing was rife with allusions to conflict, war and battle.[5] Male assumptions and behavioural models were shaped in an era when many men were returning from war, which meant women were returning to their traditional domestic role after having stepped up to work when men were in service.[6]

Despite this, the domestication of women still held as the standard and as late as the 1970s many men were still 'in charge' of all important family matters — determining where they would live, whether she worked and how property would be managed.[7] And so the scene had been set in business: men were in charge, operating through their perspective, and women fell into line behind and below them.

THINGS HAVE CHANGED – OR HAVE THEY?

There have been fundamental changes since that era, especially in women's lives. The contraceptive pill gave women the choice to decide on their own fertility. Women joined the workforce, received equal access to education and enjoyed many opportunities they were previously denied.

Today women's lives and work have expanded in many different ways. For example, many women spend their twenties completing university or further education and establishing a career.[8] Compare this with the first half of the twentieth century, when women often worked for a short time in their twenties, only to leave the workforce to take up their main domestic role.[9]

Up until the last half century, women had a family income (that is, a husband's income) and a different job description. Some of these women who raised children in their twenties and thirties were empty-nesters by their late forties and fifties.[10] Today some women in their early to mid forties are only just starting to build their family. Now there are no 'norms' for when women have children, and the median age for mothers in Australia is 31.[11]

Some women who don't have children by age 31 spend the decade building their professional lives and cementing relationships. When I was 30 I was one of 3 per cent of women globally in the position of creative director. I watched my male bosses make the decision not to start a family, or just to avoid family responsibility by choosing a partner who would dedicate her life to staying at home and caring for the kids. This certainly made 'see it, be it' a big ask.

So in my thirties I consciously made a calculation. I knew that if I were to continue working with an agency, the demands on my time, at an average of 60 hours a week, would probably make having children impossible. The point is that there are many more women like me, delaying childbirth until later into their thirties while they establish their own business or protect their careers without fearing that 'being a mum' might make them appear less committed to the job or to a C-suite position.

Some women in positions that command great salaries but demand heavy time commitments are delaying having children until much later, even into their forties. At the same time, many others are choosing to leave the safety of full-time employment and start their own business, working on their own terms, so they can juggle the commitments of business and family life.

Just over one-third of all Australian business owners are women, and this number is trending upwards each decade.[12]

WOMEN WANT MORE

A global research study of 12000 women from 20 countries by the Boston Consulting Group (BCG) titled 'Women Want More' found that balancing the competing demands of home, career and family was one of women's greatest dilemmas.[13]

Importantly, businesses that want to remain viable and competitive must look for ways to solve women's time challenges and cater to their unmet needs and to market gaps.

For employers, this raises challenges and demands change. To attract female talent, you need to rewrite the workforce contract to include co-parenting leave, flexible hours and off-site work opportunities. Whatever the brand, and whether business-to-business or business-to-consumer is your focus, you must find new ways of attracting, relating, creating and communicating with women.

The new choices men and women are making around family and career have opened up a great opportunity for addressing these points of tension and creating solutions that suit these new market needs.

This is where you come in.

Addressing women's different and evolving needs presents challenges and opportunities, forcing us to reassess and relearn the foundations on which businesses operate today.

Much has been written on this topic, yet the BCG study found that women still feel dissatisfied with services, products and market choices across most industries. These are just the top ten areas of dissatisfaction:

1. home remodelling
2. work clothes
3. home cleaning
4. physicians
5. lingerie
6. hospitals
7. cars
8. insurance
9. dress-up clothing
10. cosmetics.

A compilation of results from different studies that was used at a 2015 marketing-to-women conference in the United States highlighted some of the frustrations women have with brands and business[14]:

- 40 per cent of women do *not* identify with the women they see in ads
- 90 per cent of parents are concerned about the lack of female role models in TV programming
- 91 per cent of women claim advertisers don't understand them
- 59 per cent feel misunderstood by food marketers
- 66 per cent feel misunderstood by healthcare marketers
- 74 per cent feel misunderstood by automotive marketers
- 84 per cent feel misunderstood by investment marketers
- 50 per cent say they want more green choices
- 37 per cent are more likely to pay attention to brands that are committed to environmental causes.

These results highlight the need for every global business to support deeper research with a gender-specific focus. Such research must place gender intelligence front and centre, especially in a market that serves both sexes.

Traditional business models for the customer of the future, the female customer and the economy of women have become outdated and flawed.

THE WO-MAN ALGORITHM

In the late 1990s, futurist Faith Popcorn had mouths agape with her groundbreaking predictions about how brands could 'click' with consumers of the future in her first book, *Clicking*.[15] Two years later she followed up with *Eve-olution: The eight truths of marketing to women*.[16] It was through these books that I first learned how the female perspective is different from the male perspective, and how men's and women's experiences of brands differ. This is how I came to realise that we need to change the traditional paradigms in business.

Before I launched Australia's first 'marketing-to-women' agency, I spent many nights Googling the search string 'marketing, women, advertising'. Most pages were dominated by escort agency and prostitution services — put together, the three terms seemed to be synonymous with the sex trade. I was crestfallen. In 2003, a time when we had supposedly come such a long way, it was depressing to

Google and the Google logo are registered trademarks of Google Inc., used with permission.

find those search terms still led to page after page that objectified and sexualised women in order to sell 'adult entertainment' to men rather than respecting and celebrating women's importance as a financially independent, and massive, market opportunity.

Was that really the only information available to me 15 years into my marketing and advertising career? Is that all the world of business and consumers had to offer on the subject of women and selling? Apparently it was.

So, more convinced than ever that we needed to turn the world around, I continued my quest for knowledge on identifying and meeting the needs of female consumers. The same search with the removal of the word 'woman' turned up pages and pages of marketing and advertising genius. Yet two letters, *wo*, tacked on the front of the word 'man' completely changed the algorithm.

Fast forward to now. Thankfully we have more choices today. While it still isn't considered significant enough to be recognised at the library as a defined area of interest, there are many more specialists who have taken it up as a serious subject for scholarship.

A review of the online bookstore Booktopia turned up 4486 books in a general marketing search and just six in a refined search for books written on 'marketing to women'. Google 'marketing books' today and you'll find one in 30 written by a woman. Online site Mashable's 'top ten marketing books you must read in 2017' are all written by men.

We might ask:

Why haven't we made more progress with meeting the needs of the female consumer?

IT'S A $28 TRILLION QUESTION

In 2009 a *Harvard Business Review* report on the aforementioned Boston Consulting Group study found that women then controlled $20 trillion, projected to rise to $28 trillion by 2014. No current figure has been published, but we can assume that it has continued to trend upwards.[17] So, in financial terms, women as spenders are a global aggregate market worth about twice India and China combined.

While there will be nuances, the facts and statistics generally show that women are the biggest and fastest growing consumer economy.[18] Women's incomes have made them increasingly significant financial contributors to the household, and they have risen to become equal if not the dominant decision makers within the family.[19] McKinsey Global showed that removing the pay gap between men and women would add trillions of dollars to annual global GDP, making women an even more powerful economy to embrace and understand.

Women are your core customers, the most influential consumers and the primary shoppers and influencers across most sectors, from food to pharmaceuticals, computers and cars.

Furthermore, numerous global and regional education studies confirm that women account for the majority of university graduates,[20] which means the emerging graduate pool is deluged with female talent, making 'pipeline' issues a thing of the past.

The economic and educational empowerment of women is boosting the demand for diversity, and women's economic power is set to increase exponentially.

Tapping into this market is like having all the odds stacked in your favour. It really is a no-brainer.

GETTING HER BUY-IN

According to global studies made available by online source Sheconomy and sourced to Greenfield Online for Arnold's Women's Insight Team, women account for 85 per cent of all consumer purchases, including[21]:

- 91 per cent of new homes
- 66 per cent of PCs
- 92 per cent of vacations
- 80 per cent of health care
- 65 per cent of new cars
- 89 per cent of bank accounts
- 93 per cent of food
- 93 per cent of OTC pharmaceuticals
- 58 per cent of total online spending.

A LIGHT ON BLIND SPOTS

It seems that business paradigms have yet to be transformed, and many female consumers remain underwhelmed and disappointed with the traditional thinking, behaviour and options available to them.

The BCG 'Women Want More' study[22] revealed that most women feel very under-served in the marketplace. The same kind of unconscious bias that has disadvantaged women in many ways in the workforce and in visible leadership roles is echoed at the consumer level. Women still feel they are invisible and underestimated. Even if they are acknowledged, they do not feel their needs are considered fully. Work, home and family pressures and their interplay are inadequately understood by business.

Complicating any discussion on gender is the noise about gender diversity. Where does it fit into the discussion on economic opportunity? We will return to the subject of diversity and its relevance to leveraging female consumers for greater business success. With the economic importance of the female market well established, it is clear that both women and men will play a pivotal role in redeveloping businesses of the future.

And this is a golden opportunity for you as a business decision maker!

As we saw earlier, when asked about their feelings towards advertising, many women feel misunderstood and ignored by advertisers and marketers.[23] And while exact figures have been questioned, it leaves no room for doubt that a serious problem exists. Perhaps it reflects an underlying rejection of an antiquated business model so dominated by the past, with its lack of gender diversity and overabundance of rigid traditions, that it remains reluctant to address its relationship with women who feel invisible and underserved.

BECOME CONSCIOUS **OF THE BIAS**

Gender stereotyping can be reprogrammed, and it may indeed be eradicated in the future, but today we are still living in a world where there is pink Lego for girls and yellow Lego for boys, where McDonald's happy meals have 'boy toys' and 'girl toys', where women are the home-makers and men are the home-owners.

We have come a long way, with more women in the workforce creating a different kind of role modelling for girls, but we are still strongly influenced by traditional gender roles and raising women who 'nest' and men who 'hunt'. Yes, gender roles are shifting and responsibilities in the home are more often shared, but there are generations of built-in DNA still to address.

A fireman can feel the heat underfoot and know how long he has before the ceiling will collapse, because he has put in his 10 000 hours on the job and all that experience makes it seem like second nature. This is the almost instinctual factor that Malcolm Gladwell writes about in his book *Blink*.[24] The same instinct develops when it comes to household functioning and what girls learn growing up.

From birth, girls model how to become the CEO of the home. They draw on the same instinct or second nature their mother had. More unusually, the primary caregiver will have been male and acknowledgement of this is implicit. The traditional gender patterns remain, and men and women taking equal responsibility for home admin, groceries, cleaning, decorating, tidying and cooking may still be generations away.

The BCG 'What Women Want' research highlighted the difference in household responsibility between men and women, with women putting in significantly more hours of labour in the home than men.[25] The global average showed that at least 40 per cent of men rarely or never help their wives with household chores.[26]

When I was young, shopping for my family was something I did week in, week out. Supermarket shopping became my weekend enter-tainment with Mum, and by age 12 I was sent off on my own with a blank cheque and a budget of $120 to do the grocery shop for the whole family. Implicit in my consumer knowledge are all the preferences and experiences ingrained from childhood. From the time Mum pushed me around in the trolley aged just one to my more responsible ventures as a young teenager, my impressions were gradually taking form around store design and shelf placement, merchandising techniques and customer behaviour. Modelling their mother, girls learn these tasks and clock up a lot of flying hours by the time they are independent adult consumers.

Boys my age, meanwhile, were outside exploring the world on a bike or skateboard or playing competitive sports. Every male and female will have their own version of 'engendering gender', but suffice to say that because of inbuilt gender differences — DNA, hormones and brain chemistry — coupled with the social conditioning, women do have an instinctive insight into other female consumers.

By this I don't mean to suggest that you must hire only women, or that employing only women will solve all your business problems, or even that you must be a woman to understand and communicate with women, as you will see later in the book. However, this affiliation is a strength if you allow it to be and if you build a female-lensed business culture. This is a ripe opportunity that has yet to be recognised or leveraged by business today.

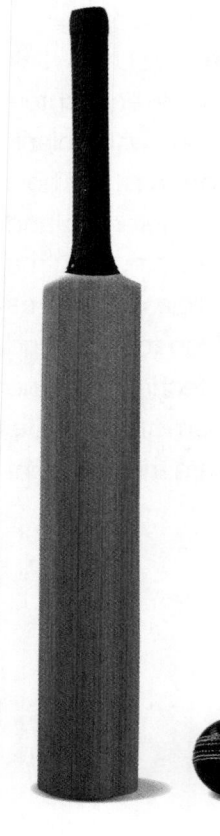

I took on my first paid job when I was 14. I was busy working in a pharmacy earning money and learning about retail, selling everything from laundry powder to lipstick, while my mates spent their free time competing in the sporting arena. I was learning to understand buyer behaviour and different customer needs while they were honing physical games of strategy, aggression and conquest.

I loved helping women customers make decisions and working with them to deliver what they were really looking for. Some women were looking for hope, others for products to fill a void; some just wanted a short cut to make the daily demands of life easier. And this is where the 'flying hours' and Blink theory first manifested for me.

In the future, as more men take on equal responsibility for raising their children, gender stereotyping will be less prevalent, but for now we are still dealing with the legacy of gender conditioning. Recent studies have shown that businesses that embrace greater gender diversity have also implemented paternity leave and parenting policies.[27] Such progressive initiatives, which often seem to go hand in hand, are bringing about the kinds of systemic changes that will see improvement across company cultures at all levels.

FROM REJECT ━━━━━━━━━━━━

As more books on the power of the female economy emerge, more science is being applied to this economic opportunity. Yet despite these findings and attempts at educating businesses, there is little movement across business as a whole. We are still seeing only half the picture, whether because of a lack of education, an ingrained attachment to traditional practices or simply a lack of focus.

When it comes to women, there is often a closed loop of old-school leaders at the top dismissing or discounting the value that gender insights offer. Or, for no other reason than classic unconscious bias, they are just not seeing it at all. As one CEO told me, 'When the customers start asking for it, we'll start thinking about it, but right now why would we change the way we've always approached our business?'

When business interfaces with the consumer, it is making an impact and impression on its audience through the way the product or service delivers, how sales staff treat customers, the performance of its call centres, and the way advertising and communications deliver its messages.

The gender nuances evident here are going to affect the way your customer starts, continues or ends a relationship with your brand. If you reveal a strong male-lensed orientation even though you have a large female audience, you are missing out on important relationships and results.

TO RESULTS

All people and businesses exist somewhere on the continuum of acceptance around how gender intelligence can unlock a growth strategy for their business.

Figure 1.1 shows what happens to our bottom line when we are educated on gender.

Looking at the figure, if you **Reject** gender in your business right now then you are avoiding the discussion entirely. I'd say reading this book is a great first step along the continuum

Figure 1.1: from reject to results

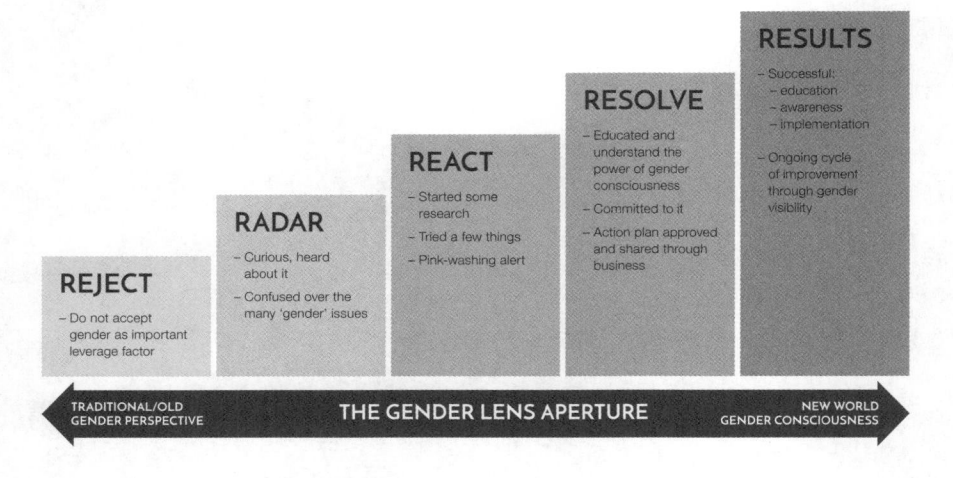

We are in a new era,
which means we need
a new attitude awareness
and approach to the
mass influencer
— women.

When gender is on your **Radar** then the people within your business have some interest in the topic but are likely confused by some of the biggest business myths, which we explore in chapter 6.

Typically, when people express an interest in talking to me they are in the **React** phase and don't want to make a wrong move. They have determined they need a new prescription for how to focus on and leverage the female market.

When businesses are armed with the **Resolve** that women are an unrealised audience opportunity, the magic starts to happen. They understand they are now entering a quest to learn how to identify the potential wealth of their audience and, looking through the female lens, the business starts to transform.

The **Results** phase is the 'centre of excellence' where the business naturally behaves in a congruent way with its females. With education and awareness, successful implementation of the female growth strategy is assured; now the business is ready to build an upward trajectory based on its new female-lensed orientation.

The day is dawning when we can no longer sweep this issue under the carpet or dismiss it as a token exercise in pink-washing.

If you believe in 'following the money', then you need to consider a fundamentally different approach. We are at a point in history when women are demanding to be recognised. Businesses that fail to look at gender through the female prism expose an underbelly of gender bias.

Outdated attitudes, an unwillingness to recognise the new changing world order, male-majority boards and executive teams — none of these established practices will move the needle. To see the full picture as it exists today, we must acknowledge and utilise both gender lenses. Homogenous or biased perspectives will limit progress and the potential to increase customer loyalty, average spend and market share.

Simply put, we will make more money by consciously servicing our biggest consumer. This means opening our eyes and recognising our blind spots, which is what we will explore in the next chapter.

CHAPTER 2

ARE YOU BLIND?

Given the numerical dominance of women consumers, you'd be right in thinking organisations should be pretty gender aware already. After all, advertisers and marketers are responsible for knowing their target audiences inside and out, right?

Yet in my first 13 years of working in advertising agencies back in the 1990s, I saw and experienced firsthand so much bias, harassment and poor behaviour that it motivated me to create my own agency where 'female vision' and basic respect for women were fundamental values. It seemed to me that if this wasn't how companies thought about and treated the women inside their organisation, how could they possibly empathise with women outside the business?

LACK OF INTELLIGENCE

The advertising industry (like broader business) attracts its fair share of clever men and women yet they continue to lack the nuance of gender-intelligence to engage with evolved modern women, whether in their workforce or among their end-consumers.

In the United States in 2016, Gustavo Martinez, CEO of global advertising agency J. Walter Thompson, was left little choice other than to resign after a young woman complained about his behaviour.[1] She alleged that he had made racially insensitive comments, suggested women needed a 'good raping' and had grabbed a female employee by the throat 'as a joke'.[2]

It's a question of ethics and gender blindness across global industries and businesses, not just in advertising.

Leaders from J. Walter Thompson's parent company, WPP, claimed this was an isolated incident, yet stories flooding in from women employees painted a very different picture. In fact, it prompted a research piece, 'Elephant on Madison Avenue',[3] from The 3% Conference, who champion diversity, creativity and profitability in advertising. In this study, 54 per cent of respondents reported having been subjected to unwanted sexual advances, 88 per cent of them from a colleague, 70 per cent from a superior and 49 per cent from a client. Yet only one in three filed a complaint with their company. In addition, 83 per cent of women in advertising have witnessed sexist behaviour at off-sites or conferences, and 91 per cent of women have encountered demeaning comments within the 'bro-culture' in which they work.

Being excluded from important meetings in order to deny them information or opportunity to contribute was a tactic reported by 58 per cent of women, and 60 per cent said they were less well compensated than their male peers.

In mid 2016, high-profile ad veteran Kevin Roberts, of Saatchi & Saatchi fame, was earning $3 million for his role as a network 'coach'.[4] In an interview with a journalist where he claimed that women in advertising lacked 'vertical ambition',[5] he took particular aim at Cindy Gallop, an outspoken champion of women in the advertising industry. While he claimed she stood up for women only to 'grab the headlines', his own outdated views of women made the front pages globally, which later sealed his fate.[6]

Today the proportion of female creative directors globally hovers around 11 per cent,[7] and not one woman was named among the top-earning agency CEOs in 2016, proving that women still face major challenges rising to the C-suite and senior ranks.[8]

But these problems are not limited to the advertising industry. The Australian Workplace Gender Equality report of 2016 showed that women in full-time employment earn almost 23 per cent less than men.[9] Just 16.3 per cent of CEOs and 28.5 per cent of key managers are women despite their making up 49.7 per cent of the workforce.[10]

The World Economic Forum's annual global gender gap report places Australia and the United States in 46th and 47th position respectively out of 144 countries.[11]

We must transform our old ways of working and operating, inside as well as outside of business, in industries and organisations of all sizes.

If you want to compete in the future and be valued by female consumers, and if you see business as a facilitator for social change, then as a leader you have no option but to begin this transformation. And it starts with the way women in the workforce are treated, and the presence of women in positions of influence.

The 3% Conference was birthed not from a sense of fairness or affirmative action. It came from a far less PC impulse.

Disgust.

Oh, and a little bit of greed.

You see, for years in California, I ran an ad agency specialising in marketing-to-women and saw the writing on the wall. Purchase influence, early tech adoption, wealth amassment: all tilting towards women. Yet the ad agency business (from which I hail) remained stubbornly male. I was disgusted with the way female consumers were overlooked entirely in ads or insulted by one-dimensional depictions (the buzz-kill wife! the domestic drill-sergeant! the sex-pot girlfriend!). And I was aware of the fortune awaiting any brand smart enough to figure out how to take female consumers seriously.

Knowing that the ad business (largely run by white dudes) had little impetus to change, I created something highly persuasive: community. Event by event, the 3% Conference built a community of creatives ready to reimagine a world where more women make media so that media makes more of women. Social media amplified our voices and, 16 events in 16 cities later, men are on board. Clients are on board. Tech companies are on board. Pretty much anyone with innovation at their hub understands our drumbeat:

Diversity = Creativity = Profitability.

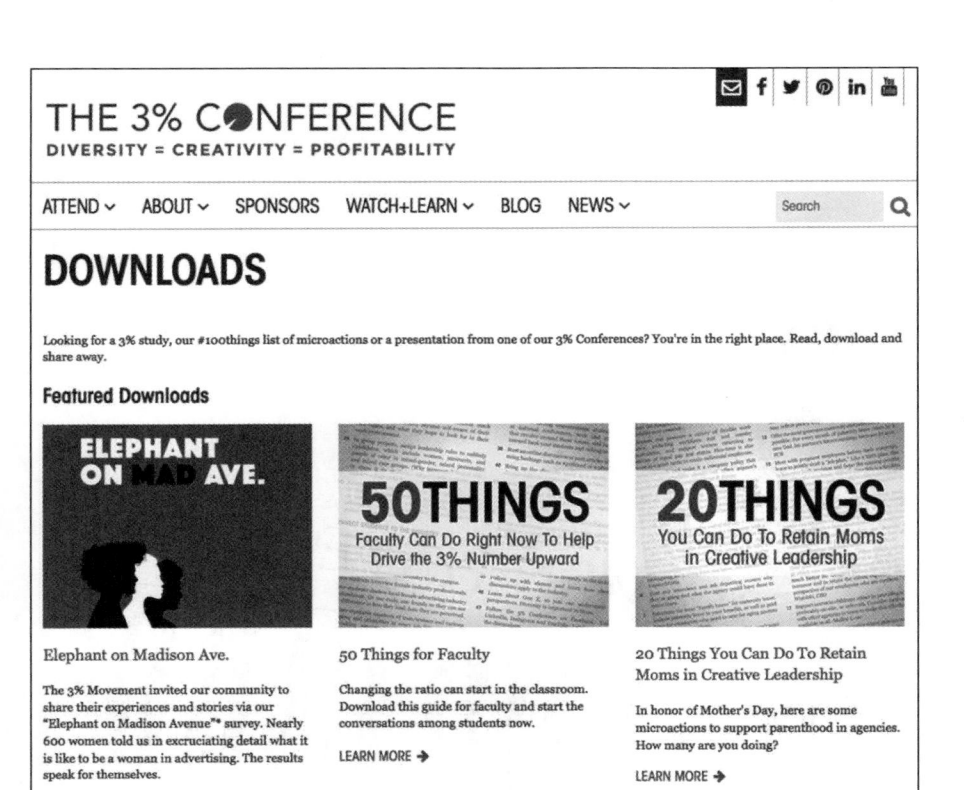

What I've learned over the past six years is this: lead with data. Numbers talk. Build community, city by city. Invite everyone into the conversation. Be optimistic and report back. Female creative directors are now up to 11.5 per cent (from 3 per cent) and we're not stopping until we near or pass 50 per cent.

A
♠

DO MEN HAVE THE

TRUMP CARD

IN BUSINESS?

♠
A

In the 2016 US presidential campaign between Hillary Clinton and Donald Trump, Trump's derogatory commentary on women stirred up important conversations and generated a collective 'fourth-wave feminist' outcry from women and men all over the world.[12]

Former first lady Michelle Obama spoke publicly of Donald Trump's language as 'cruel', 'hurtful' and 'frightening' for women.[13] The presidential candidate gave voice to how many alpha males in power think and behave. In one captured comment he boasted of how he would 'grab them by the pussy'.[14]

So if this sort of attitude reflects the thinking of the majority of male leaders at the top responsible for running businesses that sell to women, there's clearly a need for urgent improvement on many levels, in particular with regard to empathy and insightful understanding of women's needs and expectations.

Michelle Obama has continued to speak out against these backward attitudes, most recently in June at Apple's annual 2017 #WWDC conference. To an enormous audience of tech entrepreneurs she said, 'Women are in charge of everything. We buy everything. We make most decisions in the household. Who are you marketing to? ...'[15]

But it's not just the chauvinism and bias in business and politics that demand to be challenged. In 2014, Dr Alyson McGregor addressed an audience at TedxProvidence on the gender bias that has cost women's lives.[16] It's reported that the withdrawal of 80 per cent of the pharmaceutical drugs from the market has followed evidence of side effects in women. This is explained by the fact that most clinical trials focus exclusively on male cells. Female cells are ignored.[17]

Using the example of Zolpidem, prescribed for sleeping difficulties, Dr McGregor reported that many women may have had too much of this drowsy drug still in their system while driving a vehicle the next day. Only after the drug had been in market for some years was it found that women metabolise the drug at a different rate from men. A lethal cocktail of careless oversights saw its release to market without adequate research! McGregor asks us to consider how the clinical research was limited to males. The answer? 'It was the way it had been done historically.'

The prevailing attitude has been that men are the standard size and the go-to model on which we make decisions and set norms and rules.

There is an urgent need to uncover these patterns and begin to implement change in what gender intelligence looks like. From the way we view sex and gender in commerce and business; to the ways in which it operates with women not only internally, but externally too. The way business and brand present to consumers and to society at large needs to be re-examined from the vantage point of female empowerment.

When you consider how business attitudes and actions translate in the way the world operates, then seizing the opportunity to connect with a female market is a necessary new growth strategy.

BLIND SPOTS

Most organisations right across society unconsciously see the world through a male filter.

BUSINESS HER-ITAGE

It is important to review how history has dictated our current paradigm. Historically, women's place was in the home, cooking, cleaning and reproducing. Women's Darwinian role was as the nurturer who served the needs of the household and facilitated the smooth running of family life. Men worked in coalmines, on farms and in village craft shops in pre-industrial days, and in factories and mills during the industrial boom, when new economic opportunities in town gave rise to financial and commercial businesses offering all scopes of work for men determined to pursue a lifelong career.

We can appreciate the impact on women of the post-industrial global economy and how they have increasingly entered the workforce across the past century. Yet the embedded women-at-home, men-at-work programming still affects how some behave and think about business now.

In a fascinating article titled '"Vital industry" and women's ventures: Conceptualizing gender in twentieth century business history',[18] Kathy Peiss described the era when most male executives were perfectly comfortable with excluding women completely from positions of power.

Women who entered employment in the early twentieth century after the gains won courageously by the Suffragettes usually became shopgirls, fashion buyers, telephonists and typists. Few women had the opportunity to break into serious professions or big business. In 1935, as Peiss recounts, Archibald MacLeish wrote about this in *Fortune* magazine. The absence of women in business that he observed only reinforced his view that their place was in 'general business' but not in the 'vital industries'. Nearly one hundred years later, a *Harvard Business Review* article listed the 100 top-performing CEOs, only two of whom were women.[19]

MacLeish described how women had pursued business in areas that were more feminine: fashion, cosmetology, department store buying and women's magazines. These were not, in his view, 'fundamental, indisputable and corporate, mass-production industry, or technological innovation and business strategy'.[20] They were 'feminine pursuits' that somehow lacked the legitimacy of the more serious masculine areas of employment. 'Elizabeth Arden is not a potential Henry Ford,' he suggested. 'She is Elizabeth Arden, a career in itself but not a career in industry.'

These kinds of views on the essential nature of women and their place in business, perpetuated over time, highlight the need to transform our traditional masculine lens on business.

The persistent sexual divisions of workplace employment demonstrate that we have a problem that still manifests today in fundamental misunderstandings about modern women in the real world. Today's businesses need to ensure they are not missing their opportunities to earn the female dollar.

We have inherited a long workforce history that was built for men, by men, so a strong gender bias in favour of the blokes in business is no surprise. There will be times when male privilege reigns supreme and using a wrecking ball to dismantle it will not bring about solutions fast enough.

We must use intelligence and determination to make this world right for both genders.

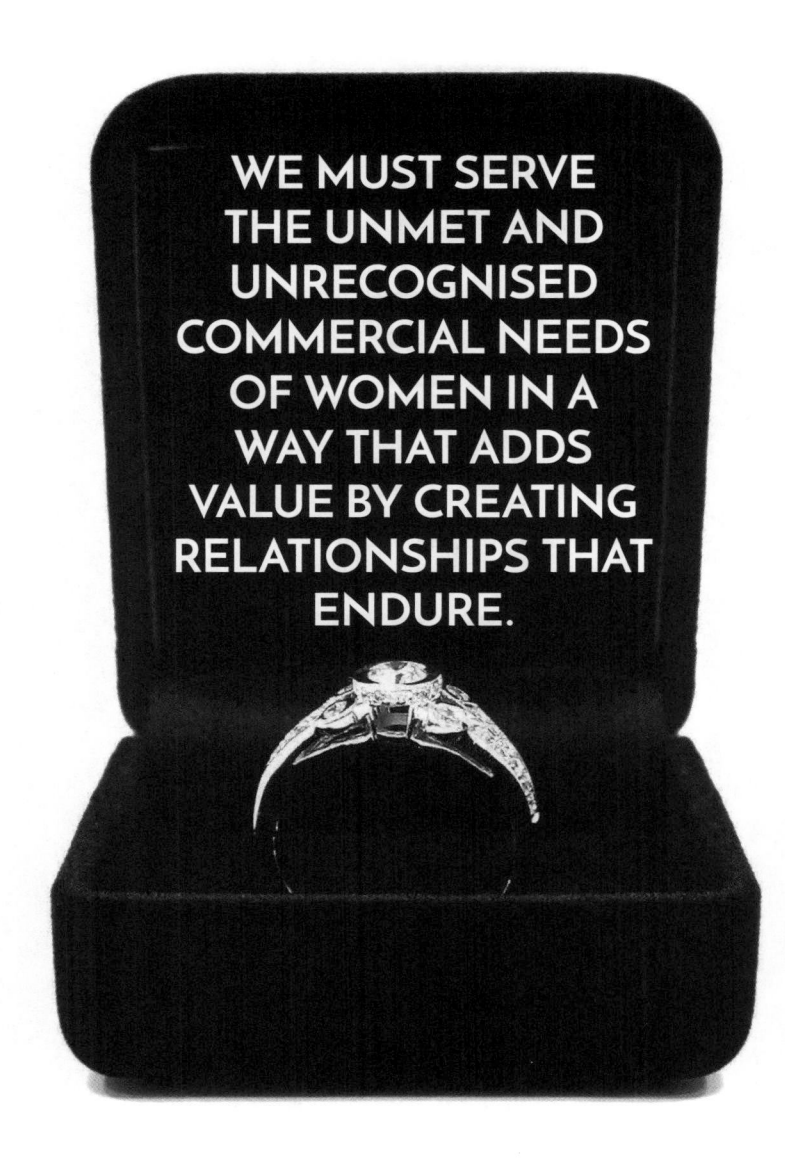

WE MUST SERVE
THE UNMET AND
UNRECOGNISED
COMMERCIAL NEEDS
OF WOMEN IN A
WAY THAT ADDS
VALUE BY CREATING
RELATIONSHIPS THAT
ENDURE.

E	1
F P	2
T O Z	3
L P E D	4
P E C F D	5
E D F C Z P	6
F E L O P Z D	7
D E F P O T E C	8
L E F O D P C T	9
F D P L T C E O	10
F E Z O L C F T D	11

WHERE ARE YOUR BLIND SPOTS?

Still not sure whether your organisation is using a male or female lens? Answer these questions honestly to find out.

1. What percentage of your entire market is identified with the female consumer spend? What is your cost per acquisition, male to female? What is your average spend, male to female?

2. How many men do you have in your whole organisation — from top-level executives to administration? How many women? How many men are on your board? How many women? What is your staff attrition rate for males versus females? Why do you think this is?

3. How do you target males? Females? How effective is this targeting? How do you segment your audience?

4. How much is the female economy worth to you, and how much are you missing out on because of your answers above?

PRESENTING THE DATA...

Diversity is better for business. Plain and simple. This topic has been much discussed by executives for at least a decade.

Countless in-depth studies have shown that diversity in all forms, including around gender, race and disability, will yield upwards of 15 per cent greater returns.[21]

In 2015 McKinsey published a study, 'Diversity Matters', that examined data sets for 366 public companies across a range of industries in Canada, Latin America, the UK and the United States. Companies in the top quartile for gender diversity were 15 per cent more likely to achieve financial returns above their respective national industry median. Companies in the bottom quartile on gender, ethnicity and race were statistically less likely to achieve above-average financial returns than the average companies in the data set — they are lagging, not leading.

In the UK, greater gender diversity on the senior executive team corresponded to the highest uplift in the data set: for every 10 per cent increase in gender diversity, EBIT rose by 3.5 per cent.

Diversity translates to innovation, improved outcomes and bigger profit.

In 2016, the Peterson Institute for International Economics in collaboration with EY produced a study titled 'Is Gender Diversity Profitable?'[22] It examined 22 000 public companies across 91 different countries in 2014, about half of which had no female executives. Moreover 60 per cent had no women on their boards and fewer than 5 per cent had female CEOs.

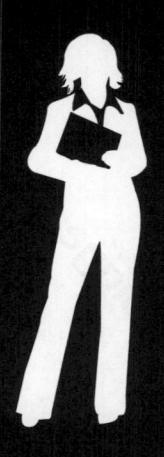

Evidence from the Peterson study found that companies with at least 30 per cent female leaders had net profit margins up to 6 per cent higher than companies with no women in the top ranks.

A *Catalyst* study in 2007 titled 'The bottom line: Corporate performance and women's representation on boards'[23] found that Fortune 500 companies with at least three female directors have a:

- 42 per cent higher return on sales

- 53 per cent higher return on equity

- 66 per cent higher return on invested capital.

The researchers also found stronger-than-average results on financial performance where at least three women serve on a company board.

The decision to change the old guard is not as simple as publishing great studies, even when greater profitability could be an outcome for a business. It means taking action to get more women promoted through the ranks and serving on boards. As these gender diversity studies show, the financial performance of companies can be quantified across most sectors, as can the benefits of deliberately including more women in their boards of directors.

The bottom line is that you are more likely to outperform your competitors if you have females on your board.

So with objective, evidence-based results like these, why are the conclusions not being embraced? If the financial[24] benefits of gender diversity apply to most business sectors, why is this not being translated into action everywhere? How can it be that boards furnished with these facts do not insist that more women are immediately promoted or employed in senior ranks?

BLIND SPOTS

MORE THAN BUMS AROUND THE BOARDROOM

If the boards themselves were to take control of the issues we might see faster progress. In an article in *The New Statesman*, 'The rise and fall of Default Man', Grayson Perry compares the outcry against positive discrimination to 'the wail of someone who is having their privilege taken away. For talented black, female and working-class people to take their just place in the limited seats of power, some of those Default Men are going to have to give up their seats.'

Surely it would make sense to put more seats around the table than expect those who have earned their seat, whether through privilege or hard work, to give up their place? Boards can have as many members as they need. In recent times the smaller board was favoured in the belief that consensus decision making was easier to achieve. Some have argued that it would cost too much to add extra seats, but this feels like an excuse to maintain the status quo.

Some of the most significant changes in today's fast-paced world of innovation have come unexpectedly and at unprecedented speed. It took over 20 years for radio to build up a large commercial listening audience, yet just one week for game app Pokémon Go to eclipse Tinder and Twitter in numbers of daily users.[25] This illustrates that markets in this age are volatile and change can rapidly go viral.

Creating diversity is going to mean making some intelligent decisions for outcomes that produce longer-term profitability and true survival for business.

And herein lies the dilemma facing business. Once male business leaders understand that there is only a financial upside in catering to the unmet, unrealised and undervalued dollars of the female consumer, the tipping point will be reached fast. We can only hope that both men and women will soon appreciate the benefits of having a very clear and unobstructed view, with the blind spots fully illuminated.

AS THE INFLUENCE OF THE FEMALE CONSUMER GROWS, COMPANIES THAT HIRE WOMEN AT BOARD AND C-SUITE LEVEL WILL BE SET UP FOR FUTURE SUCCESS.

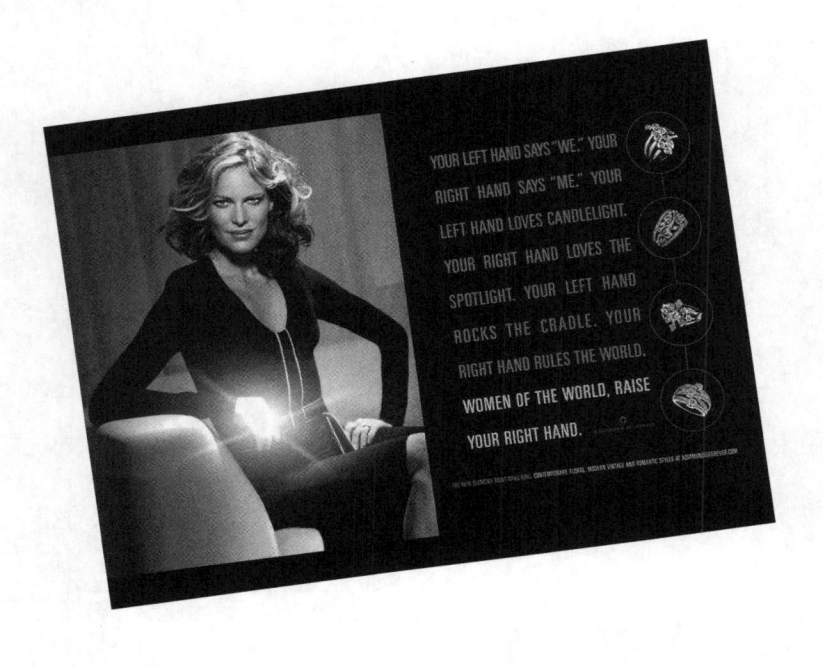

THE RESULT OF GETTING IT RIGHT

It is in the financial interest of any organisation to make the commitment in time, energy and budget to ensure that we all learn to see the world clearly and free from bias.

Companies with gender-equal or gender-neutral audiences should not look at male *or* female but rather at male *and* female, separately.

Look at De Beers, the US diamond company that invented the engagement ring narrative that had men bestowing them as precious gifts of esteem to their brides-to-be.[26] Some female-lensed thinking unearthed that behaviours around matrimony and engagement had changed. With a growing population of single women, this created a great opportunity to realign their antennae to listen to what modern women were asking for. And through this process they discovered that the modern, financially independent and wealthy woman was no longer waiting for Prince Charming to embellish her finger with a diamond status symbol.

She was using her independence and her own cash to assert her worth and make her own statement, because she could afford to. This insight led to the birth of the 'right-hand ring', with advertising communicating that the left hand might say 'we' but the right-hand diamond powerfully says 'me'.[27]

With this incredibly smart positioning of the same ring, and a wonderfully ingenious insight into the psyche of enlightened women, sales increased 15 per cent. The kicker was the empathy they showed by understanding the psyche of women today.

Viewing business through the female lens means getting the right focus on the value of women both internally as a workforce asset and externally as the end user or consumer you serve. Understanding your female audience also means understanding that they are physically different from your male audience, and that this too has an impact on your business and the way you operate. We'll look at how next.

If you are in business to make more money (and we all are, right?), then the following four factors should excite and motivate you into connecting with your female audience:

1. **increased average spends, repeat business and positive word of mouth, leading to greater profits**

2. **better customer acquisition and retention, translating into customer loyalty**

3. **attraction to your business of a wider pool of talent, resulting in a more balanced workforce and a thriving culture**

4. **breakthrough innovation through diversity in opinion, culture and gender.**

CHAPTER 3

PROOF OF DIFFERENCE

Comedian Mark Gungor explains on YouTube that men possess 'boxes, compartments and a simplistic filing system for every thought process that can be easily categorised into its appropriate place'. Women, on the other hand, possess 'a system that mimics a seemingly tangled ball of wire, wound and interconnecting, wrapping around and entwined within a space that is always on and always actively searching for meaning'.

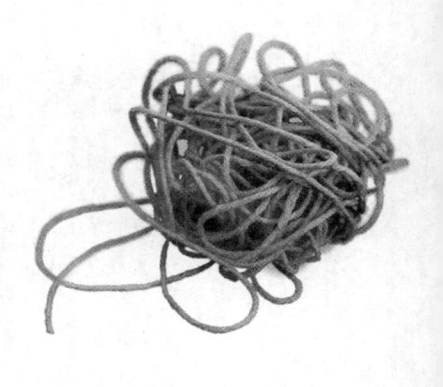

This deceptively simple (and funny) differentiation is what has made books like John Gray's *Men Are from Mars, Women Are from Venus* so popular. In our quest to understand our relationships we look to gender to explain the communication breakdowns, yet when it comes to business we discount the impact of such differences completely. We throw it away, forgetting that it is actually a key to improving not just our personal relationships but our business relationships too.

So why do so many businesses ignore such an obvious factor? Why do many of them even hide from the subject of gender, choosing to homogenise the very people they want to build a relationship with? More importantly, what would happen if we used our gender differences as a competitive advantage?

Every day men and women make different decisions about the most basic of things. Most of us follow a prescribed path that's laid out for us based on which genitals we have. Do we wear a dress or pants? Choose the female or male bathroom? Which box do we tick on a medical form? Everything we do seems to reinforce our differentness rather than our sameness.

Right now there is a lot of homogenising or 'gender whitewashing' in business. We categorise our target audience — customers, clients, stakeholders, employees — under one generic banner.

The greater our knowledge of how to engage with the masculine and feminine consumer differently, the better we can tailor our business to our audience's needs.

So why doesn't our bank, our supermarket or our phone company do the same? Why don't more tradespeople, transport companies, technology providers and tourism services cater to our different needs?

The truth is, recognising the differences across the spectrum of male and female, as perceived through the gender lens, can have a massive impact on your bottom line. The commercial considerations for better understanding gender in the marketplace are immensely important.

A principle of human-centred design is called 'designing to the edges'. It's about providing inclusivity outside the lowest common denominator or 'average'.[1] Products are designed to embrace the extremes, meaning they must be flexible and versatile enough to suit people in the market who are outside the 'norm'. Research on gender impacts in advertising shows that when you design for people at one extreme, you will also better reach the people at the other.

Gender now covers a broad spectrum with many nuances. In recent years we have become more aware and accepting of people outside traditional gender norms. I am often asked how marketers work with such people or groups. It's a great question.

Put simply, some men are inclined to more feminine traits, while some women are inclined to more masculine ones. Which gender they identify with is not actually an issue. The important thing is to connect with a gender, regardless of what their sexual orientation or preference is.

Businesses must learn how to communicate and engage with consumers, whether they are black or white, gay or straight, male, female or fluid, without the limiting perspective of a single generic, traditional male lens. By relating to people on a deeper and more meaningful level (especially if they are women!), you are more likely to foster a positive and long-lasting brand relationship.

Y CHANGE?

Right from the get-go, when human life is forming, our brain starts out female.[2] Only when the sperm carries the Y chromosome will the developing fetus become male. Mother Nature (excuse the gendered term) has her own plans for the differentiation of our species.

Testosterone and oestrogen have a big influence on how the brain develops. The size, shape and functionality of male and female brains are surprisingly different. Women have a thicker *corpus callosum*, facilitating the exchange of signals between left and right hemispheres. Men have a thicker right hemisphere and a larger cerebellum, which facilitates problem solving of spatial issues.

Science confirms that we communicate differently. Dr Louann Brizendine, who has written two books about these differences, concludes that our sex influences our listening skills, ability to communicate, vision, response to language, needs and decision making throughout our life.

Advances in medical technology have helped us to understand the brain. In neuroscience, MRI scans and imaging have shown different patterns in male and female brains as they respond to different stimuli.

Studies have shown that different areas of our brains light up when we are read the same passage of text.[3] In problem solving, women and men call on different parts of their brains to answer the same question.[4]

The male brain

The female brain

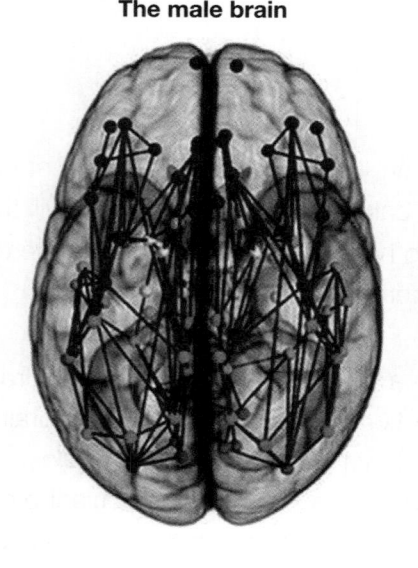 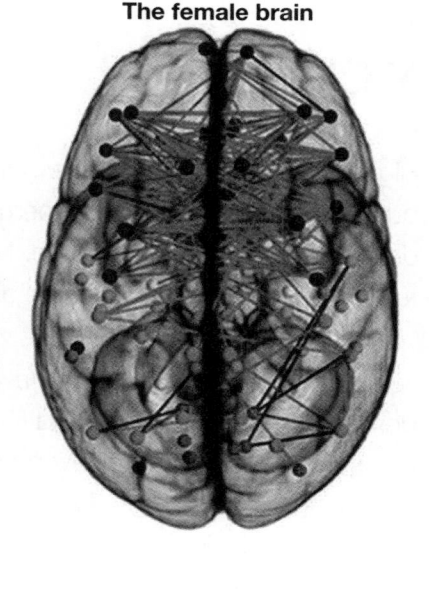

While we'd need a PhD in brain biochemistry to appreciate the different impacts of genetic wiring, table 3.1 shows some examples of how males and females tend to develop and deal with decisions and situations differently.

Once we accept that men and women think and act in fundamentally different ways, we can use these differences to better connect with each gender both within businesses and in the marketplace.

Table 3.1: common gender differences[5]

	MALE RESPONSE	FEMALE RESPONSE
Life meaning	Compete, assert, win	Create ideal world, nest, nurture
Early behaviour	Drawn to things: mechanics, functionality, machines	Drawn to people: dolls, house, relationship dynamics
Listening, communicating brain function	Neurons are activated on one side of brain	Neurons on both sides of brain are activated
Innate reaction	Action	Feeling
Response to stress	Fight and flight	Tend and befriend
Mating/reproduction	Outshine and outdo — compete	Smart and savvy choices — look for nuance
Areas of interest	Things, stuff	People, human stories
Intellectual reasoning	Linear, analytical, logical, focused	Whole-brained overview

DO YOU GET IT?

Who wears make-up, and who uses a face razor and aftershave? What about dresses and skirts? Or a suit and tie? Does Dad read the fishing mags, while Mum peruses the home interior ones? Who watches the rom coms in your family, and who likes the action/thriller flicks?

The fashion, clothing and cosmetic industries are expert at targeting men and women by creating different-sized and -shaped products, different-looking stores and carefully directed marketing ideas. The publishing industry has relied heavily on the innate differences between men and women in order to segment interests in the market. So too has Hollywood. So why don't all industries get it?

In *Why We Buy: The Science of Shopping*[6] and *What Women Want*,[7] retail expert Paco Underhill eloquently makes this point through a simple consumer story: a man and woman head to the hardware store to buy a hammer. Well, he is buying a hammer; she is buying a living-room picture wall filled with memories.

Many business sectors, such as banking, finance, food, tourism, entertainment and technology to name a few, fail to specifically target each gender through the way they market and approach customers. On the surface, the ideal consumer appears to be homogenous or genderless. This is a wasted opportunity!

We need to target males and females in business in the same way that gender-specific industries do.

Fashion and cosmetic brands generally know their audience and use specific sales tools to appeal to each gender. But if you try to connect with females through a male lens you will fail to see what they want, when they want it and how much they want to pay for it. This leads to women feeling overlooked, invisible or irrelevant to your business, which means they won't spend their time or money with you.

In 1989, Diana Williams opened Australia's first female-only gym.[8] Her idea resonated with many women who wanted their own space to work out and train in, without feeling self-conscious or nervous about being under the gaze of men. Curves (in the UK) and Contours (in the United States) also recognised this growing market, and by the mid 2000s female-only gyms were a widely accepted fitness solution. It's a business driven by the need for women to have their basic needs understood and facilitated.

The transport industry offers another classic example. Globally, hundreds of women report being harassed, both physically and verbally, in taxis every year. Some women don't feel safe getting into a car with a male stranger, for good reason. That's where the enterprising company Shebah comes in.[9] Modelled on SheTaxis, a similar service available in the United States, it's really a female-only equivalent of Uber, created by women for women. All Shebah's drivers are women, and they accept all female passengers, boys up to the age of 12, and sons travelling with their mums up to the age of 18.

When I started my company Shebah, formerly Mum's Taxi, it was clear there was an enormous gap in the market that no male-centric company had been interested in looking at. The generationally squeezed female consumer and the casual labour market of women had both been invisible to taxis and Uber.

Uber claims that 10 per cent of their drivers are women and the taxi industry is 96 per cent male (although I have never had a female cabbie). We know women take up casual work like a sponge takes up water, so why are women not driving?

Shebah aims to give a safe workplace to female drivers (there had to be a reason why I was too scared to drive for Uber and twice registered and twice backed out) and a resource for working parents, primarily women, who are looking to get help with school runs, sports training and appointments without leaving the office.

The male lens of these companies has, at a cultural level, failed to address the very serious issues of multiple sexual assaults, stalking charges, sexual harassment complaints and micro aggressions such as invasive questioning of women about their sex lives, both towards their drivers and their passengers. By ignoring the needs of women and their children, Uber have left a gap we hope to successfully fill. Wish us luck.

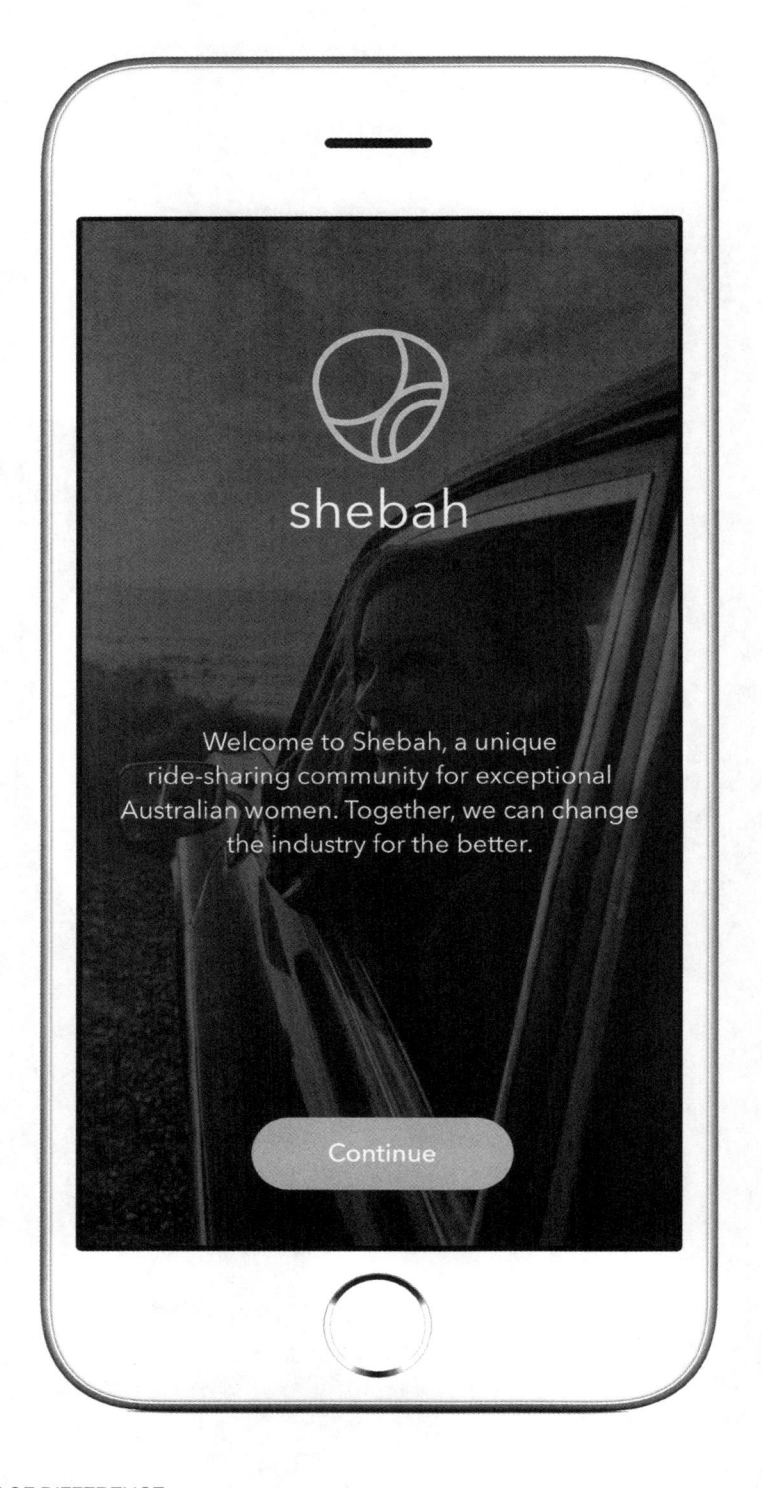

Welcome to Shebah, a unique ride-sharing community for exceptional Australian women. Together, we can change the industry for the better.

Continue

Individualising needs according to gender is not being sexist; it's being smart.

Even the hairdressing industry is cottoning on to this idea of segmenting consumers by gender. Barber shops are back, in a big way.[10] This space that caters to males only is picking up momentum around the world. Razor cuts, beard trims and eyebrow shapes are all part of the service. A more masculine environment, including spontaneous walk-ins, boutique beers, espressos and ballads on the radio, is part of the appeal.

Women, on the other hand, like hair salons where colouring, cuts and blow waves are booked in advance. Salons offer glossy mags, wi-fi, coffee, even wine for those wishing to chill out, with a complimentary mini-massage on arrival.

Which one would you rather choose?

FROM UNILEVER TO MULTI-VIEW

Unilever is parent company of the Dove soap brand, which women love for its authenticity. Their marketing campaigns for the past decade have focused on having real conversations with women about the media's unrealistic ideals of female beauty.

However, Unilever's other brands have attracted some criticism for a perceived conflict with these values. Male deodorant Lynx has broadcast past campaigns depicting unattainably beautiful women who lust after men who use their product. In one famous ad, women portrayed as angels fall out of the sky to be with men who wear Lynx.

In 2016, Unilever undertook a major global ad study. Results suggested that just 2 per cent of ads show intelligent women.[11] The research also showed:

- 40 per cent of women surveyed said they do not identify at all with the women they see in advertising

- 3 per cent of ads feature women in managerial, leadership or professional roles, with women 'disproportionately' represented in domestic roles

- 1 per cent of the ads surveyed showed women being funny — the ad industry appears to believe that the life of a woman is generally dour.

After viewing the results, Unilever CMO Keith Weed made a bold decision. Unilever pledged to remove unhelpful stereotypes from its advertising. This also included brands like Lynx, which were reinvigorated with depictions of modern men who challenge and disrupt old notions of masculinity and individuality.

The company also undertook to show women in roles that reflect the aspirations and broader, multidimensional lives of women, and that recognise the advancement of women in terms of social equality, education and sheer buying power. The proof will be in their 2017 outputs and subsequent results.

By Unilever's own admission, media and advertising specifically have been slow to reflect cultural change around gender identity and often depict an outdated view of society.

THE APPLE DOESN'T FALL FAR

In 2007, Associate Professor Michael 'Spike' Cramphorn had what he described as an Isaac Newton moment of epiphany about men and women.

While micro-analysing data drawn from 400 000 global responses to advertising from around the globe he decided to re-examine his data based on gender.

The results were illuminating[12]:

- Advertisements that were intended for both men and women were less effective than those written for a male-only or female-only audience.

- Women rated higher for engagement overall, showing that the messaging was more likely to influence the female consumer than the male consumer.

- Men and women liked different qualities in the ads, and country of origin was not relevant to the findings; that is, the consumer's gender was more important than geographic differences.

These results should have stopped many businesses in their tracks. They are reason enough to start segmenting your data right now based on gender. If men and women are so unalike in their responses to advertising, then it's time your business marketing reflected this. This means making a greater effort to understand the gender segments and to deliver more accurately on what males and females want, no matter what industry you are in.

SEGMENTATION IS KING, BUT ALSO QUEEN

Before we can micro-analyse the differences and similarities of a market, we must first macro-analyse to understand the most distinctive differentiator there is — gender.

Segmentation is a term we use when we classify consumers and markets. It helps us divide our market by common denominators, which makes it easier to identify particular customer needs.

Segmenting markets was an idea first developed early in the twentieth century.[13] In the 1980s, technological innovation gave birth to hyper-segmentation, which could identify ever narrower market segments. As more and more data has become available to us through digital analysis, we have had the opportunity to focus on and understand our audience as never before.

The four common ways of segmenting a market are:

1. behavioural
2. psychographic
3. geographic
4. demographic.

Demographic segmentation includes factors such as age, income, ethnicity, religion, family size, education and gender; however, it does not make the distinction of gender as a classification of its own. Given

how unalike we have discovered male and female behaviours, brain wiring and attitudes to be, the first step in the process of segmenting any market should be to identify the gender of the audience. Only then should further segmentation follow.

Our failure to reflect the innate differences of gendered behaviour is a massive oversight by the industry. Given that segmentation was first developed more than one hundred years ago, in an era when there were so few women in the workforce, the theory badly needs an update. We need to take into account the current conditions and especially the 'modern woman's' economic influence and impact.

This is perhaps the clearest illustration of the way the traditional male lens limits our ability to capture potential profits in today's marketplace. And it will affect your business in multiple ways, as shown in figure 3.1 (overleaf).

Figure 3.1: gender effects on business

GENDER CAN AFFECT

EXTERNALLY
The way consumers behave.
- How they feel about you
- How they choose you
- How they understand you
- How they interact with you

OPERATIONALLY
The way your business culture operates.
- Are you more masculine or feminine?
- How you design product
- How you make everyday decisions
- How you make major strategic decisions
- How you behave as a brand
- The kinds of third parties you interface with/choose

INTERNALLY
The way your staff make decisions.
- Are they more male or female lensed?
- Are they gender aware, or operating unconsciously?
- What are the approval processes— are they male or female?
- Who is/are the customers they are thinking about?

HUMAN RESOURCES
The way you hire and promote.
- Is there a dominant gender in your workforce?
- Who is making the decisions?
- Is there a policy concerning gender?
- Are staff gender-educated?

1. EXTERNALLY

Our very different brain makeup affects the way men and women interact and communicate. So whether your audience is predominantly male or female will affect how consumers relate to you. For example, if you are hoping to attract the women who influence 75 per cent of banking decisions, it would pay to develop solutions and communications that address them directly. If you are wondering why more women are not spending money at your registers, it would make sense to analyse why you are struggling in your relationship with her.

2. OPERATIONALLY

Are you gender-lensed towards the masculine or the feminine? What category norms exist and how do you compare to them? The way your products and services look, feel and relate to the end user will influence the public's perception of you. The way in which your brand is portrayed — the semiotics, such as colour, visual codes and communication language — will inform these perceptions.

3. INTERNALLY

The gender of your staff has the potential to influence the outcomes of your business focus. Will you accomplish the objectives wholeheartedly or miss them even by a few degrees? Without consciously operating with gender in mind, the marketing team may be using their own innate gender preferences and brain wiring to make decisions that will have an impact you haven't thought through.

I once worked on a project with a financial institution to target women and improve their financial literacy. After months of work the chosen strategy went through to the board for approval. The board simply did not understand the strategy; they were unconvinced by the insights and discounted the audience nuances that their working group had uncovered.

The board's unconscious bias blocked progress. The fact that they were all men further highlighted the Mars versus Venus paradigm. The project was subsequently gender-neutralised into a form the board could relate to, but as a result they failed to capture the hearts and minds of the women they were aiming at.

4. HUMAN RESOURCES

In a world shaped by bias, the gender of your team will obviously impact bottom-line potential. As the McKinsey, Catalyst and EY studies show, a more diverse team will bring a broader range of perspectives and better results to any business. The HR department is a perfect place to start this discussion about gender's impact on workplace practices.

To be absolutely clear, there are many ways that ignoring gender actually robs a business of its full potential. Every organisation should be culturally prepared to consider gender as a business-winning advantage.

Q Search

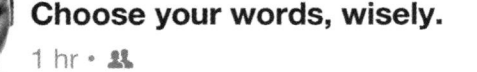

Choose your words, wisely.
1 hr · 👥

In 2016, researchers studied 65 000 Facebook users (average age 26) and their status updates.

They published their results in a report titled 'Women are warmer but no less assertive than men: Gender and language on Facebook'.[14] As the title suggests, women tended to use warmer and gentler words in their status updates compared with men, who were more likely to use expletives and argumentative and aggressive language.

The study showed that women more often focused on family life and social events and expressed positive emotions, favouring words such as 'love' and intensifiers such as 'sooo' and 'ridiculously'. Other common words were 'wonderful', 'happy', 'birthday', 'daughter', 'baby', 'excited' and 'thankful'.

Men, on the other hand, were more inclined to topics related to career, work or money. They preferred a vocabulary associated with sport, politics, competition and physical activities. Men relied on words such as 'freedom', 'win', 'lose', 'battle' and 'enemy'.

The differences were interpreted as reflecting a male inclination to objects and impersonal topics and a female inclination to psychological and social processes.

There are many studies about gender that show how our basic actions and responses are decided on by the different wiring in our heads. Clearly, then, factoring in market segmentation by gender can help us make better business decisions.

👍❤️😆   4 Comments

👍 Like   💬 Comment   ➤ Share

BLIND SPOTS

PICK YOUR BATTLE

Google the top 30 marketing books and you'll see that all of these books were written by men, and that even today many influential titles in the business and management genre reflect very masculine views of business, such as Sun Tzu's *Art of War* and Napoleon Hill's *Think and Grow Rich*.

Marketing principles were developed in a completely different era, when business planning and strategy were based on 'masculine' assumptions of competition, power and survival through 'winning'.

The masculine premise of 'winning through domination' leaves little room for the feminine premise of 'success through community'. The former is based on destroying or capturing the enemy, the latter on the impulse to improve the world for everyone.

It should come as no surprise that male-lensed business conventions often employ the language of battle. We need to remember that the people who brought 'strategy' into advertising agency methodology were ex-servicemen from the two world wars. These men used skills and tactics learned through their military experience. They naturally brought this thinking into the commercial and business world, which is why marketing talk is peppered with 'bullseyes', 'targets', 'waging campaigns' and 'guerilla activity'.

Future proofing your business means connecting to the world's largest growing audience of women, and a new approach towards creating and nurturing these relationships.

Gender is often associated with discussion of 'feminism', 'sexism' and 'equality'. It is important to distinguish between these different ideas, as all have great potential to influence the success of a business, and even of society at large.

Taxi start-up and category disruptor Uber has proven to be a runaway success. But perhaps they have grown so fast that they have overlooked essentials. Employee Susan Fowler shared her disappointment over the internal sexual harassment she encountered at Uber's head office in the United States. A failure to address internal workplace issues such as harassment, inequality and unconscious bias actually becomes a 'gender-cost' to business. A 'gender-opportunity' to business is using both a male and a female lens to better meet the inherently different needs and wants of each segment.

To do this, you really need to know who you are talking to. You need to meet her.

CHAPTER 4

MEET MODERN WOMAN

The beauty industry thought it knew everything about being beautiful, and about what women want, until Dove made a conscious decision to approach the idea from a new perspective. When they launched their Real Beauty campaign in 2004,[1] they took a stand against the conventional image of female beauty that had long been unquestioned throughout the industry. There was no longer one white, size 0, early twenties woman we should aspire to be. Instead they presented a range of women of different shapes, sizes, ages and backgrounds.

This marked a turning point in how the marketing world talked to the modern woman — or more accurately, modern *women*. The models who appeared in this campaign represented the range of women who are your target market today.

Your business, no matter what industry you are in, needs to form relationships with a multitude of different women. There is no one-size-fits-all approach.

Today's women are all different and unique; from the income they earn to their thinking and intelligence to the choices they make about where or with whom to do business. They are complex and simple, dynamic and educated. They are single, married, divorced, sisters, mums and daughters. They are business owners and entrepreneurs. Some are professional women working nine to five in an office, some are blue-collar workers, some are caregivers, some are unpaid workers in the home. Some may juggle two or even three of these roles!

It has been suggested that the twentieth century is shaping up to be 'the century of women', with further shifts away from the overt masculine bias to acceptance of a feminine perspective on the ways in which we create and think about the world. According to this perspective, women have been fitting into the patriarchal society throughout history, and perhaps we can rebalance the scales not just to see women valued differently, but to see them at all.

The housewife of a bygone era, long before the internet and smartphone, was largely disconnected from mass society. Advanced technology was a refrigerator and a television set. There was much less consumer choice, fewer products and limited exposure to the wider world. Women rarely had formal tertiary education. Men were the primary source of income. He came home to a pipe and slippers. She prepared his meals, took care of the children, did the housework and other home duties.

This 1950s image represents the archetypical woman that modern marketing was created to reach out and sell to. But the communication was in one direction only. She was relatively powerless and pliable. She had few choices and her voice was muted. She was the homemaker.

The one thing that enlightened modern women have in common is their gender. They are a richly varied and deeply nuanced group, not a homogenous body of faceless women.

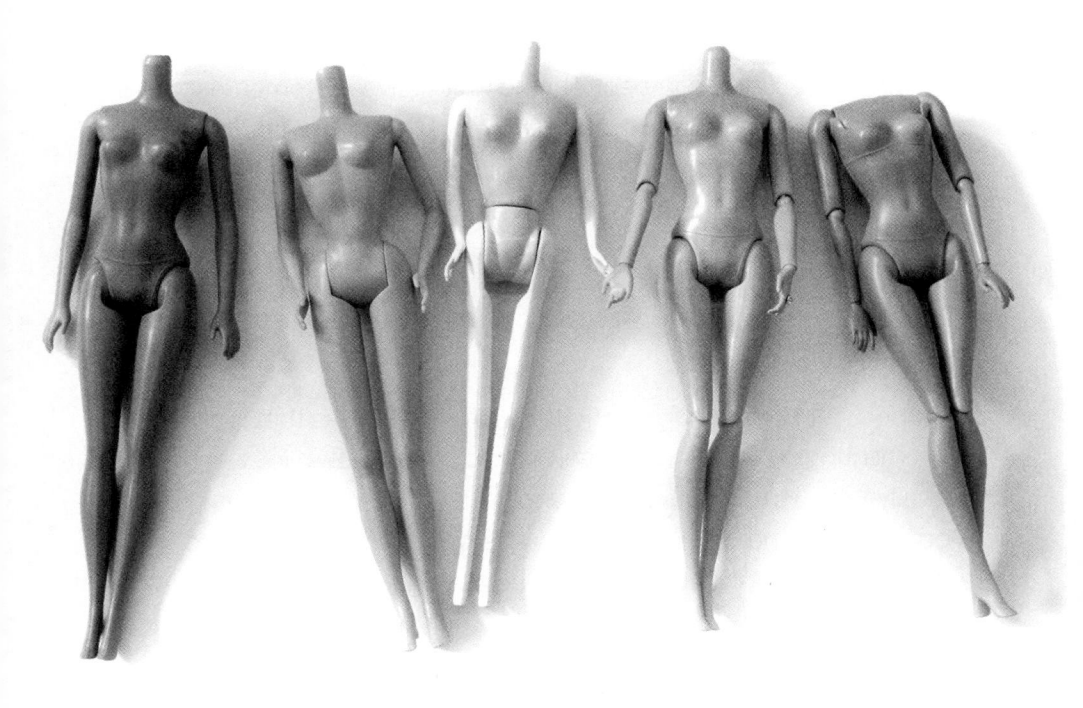

The century of women should be an anticipatory culture, looking towards the future and pre-empting the needs of women, rather than reacting to them once they have had to complain, ask, or give up and try elsewhere. This would reflect a business that is female-lensed and that purposefully acknowledges and adjusts to the new perspectives and different needs of women.

We can no longer accept a world of one size fits all. History has progressed, and women who are spending their hard-earned salaries with your business have different expectations from those your business may have built itself on in the past.

For a deeper understanding of this new worldview of women, first we need to look at the impact of time on our lives. Women especially are living in a time-poor world as they juggle the demands of work, home and family. More women work outside the home than ever before, but there is a lag-effect at play, with modern lifestyles yet to catch up with this economic and cultural change. Women have moved into a new reality but are yet to be freed from the expectations of old.

Annabel Crabb, in her book *The Wife Drought* states that while many think the juggle of work and family is a 'common joke' for women, it's actually not. 'Having a spouse who takes care of things at home is a godsend on the domestic front,' she says, 'It's a potent economic asset on the work front. And it's an advantage enjoyed — even in our modern society — by vastly more men than women.'

Acknowledging women's time poverty will lead to breakthrough innovation for business. Through understanding how women must plan, allocate and juggle their time, you will uncover solutions and strategies that can give you a market advantage over your competitors.

If your husband ever finds out

you're not "store-testing" for fresher coffee ...

...if he discovers you're still taking chances on getting flat, stale coffee ...woe be unto you! For today there's a sure and certain way to test for freshness <u>before</u> you buy

Here's how easy it is to be sure of fresher coffee

Look for the "Dome Top" Can of Chase & Sanborn. That firm, rounded top shows it's packed *under pressure*, fresh from the oven.

Just do this:

Press your thumbs against the dome top *before* you buy. If it's firm, it's fresh. If the top clicks, pressure's gone—take another. It's the one way to get the freshest coffee ever packed.

No other can lets you test!

You can't test an ordinary flat top can. Some are "leakers" that have let air in to steal freshness. But all flat top cans look alike. You can't tell which are good and which are stale.

Here's the payoff!

Sure as you pour a cup, they'll want more! For Chase & Sanborn is a glorious blend of more expensive coffees ... brought to you *fresher*. No wonder Chase & Sanborn pays a flavor dividend you won't find in any other coffee!

REGULAR GRIND
NEW PRESSURE PACKED NEW
Chase & Sanborn
COFFEE

"PRESSURE PACKED"

Chase & Sanborn

103

Giving her time back is an absolute business necessity if you want to maintain market position or knock your competition out of the market.

THE MOTHER LOAD

The squeeze on women's time in today's world has reached epidemic proportions, especially for working mothers. Many women still work by day before going home to start their 'second shift', maintaining the family home, and both are high-functioning areas of responsibility.

While increasing numbers of men are stepping up to the plate to take on more responsibility in the home, the BCG 'Women Want More' global study[2] reveals persistent deep disparities in the division of household labour, showing that the responsibility for running the home is still largely carried by women.

In its 2015 evaluation of female economic empowerment,[3] the United Nations Women site found:

- Women bear disproportionate responsibility for unpaid care work.

- Women devote one to three hours more a day to housework than men; two to ten times the amount of time a day to care (for children, elderly and the sick), and one to four hours less a day to market activities.

- In the European Union, for example, 25 per cent of women report care and other family and personal responsibilities as the reason for not being in the labour force, versus only 3 per cent of men. This directly and negatively affects women's participation in the labour force.

These figures are a powerful illustration of society's failure to catch up with the current demands of women today.

Modern woman is juggling kids, career, relationships, perhaps even an undergraduate degree. She is still doing the lion's share of work

on the domestic front while facing increasing paid-employment responsibilities. A study published in Australia in 2014 showed that the average mum enjoys just 17 minutes of 'me time' a day.[4] Like the Boston study, it found that two-thirds of women feel the household chores are not shared equally between them and their partner, and that this imbalance is making their time management a challenge.

Modern women seek out businesses that recognise these demands on her time and actively try to recognise and acknowledge her unmet needs.

Of the women surveyed, more than half the respondents reported that they had no time to themselves and about the same number agreed that this prohibited them from pursuing their own hobbies and interests. Not surprisingly, 42 per cent reported that in anything resembling spare time, they actually started planning for the next day so as to stay on top of things and avoid falling behind the next day or week, compounding a build-up of tasks.

So just how does all of this affect you as a business leader who wants to up the ante and engage the female economy?

HOW MODERN ARE YOU AND YOUR BRAND?

Ask yourself:

1. Where do we fit in her busy life? How many hours a week does she spend with us? How can we make the experience better? What needs does she have?

2. What does her ideal look like when she is interacting with us — from the sale through to her next purchase?

3. How do we fit into her community? Family? How can we fit better?

4. How can we learn to anticipate her needs so she doesn't have to ask?

5. How can we see the world through her perspective and reward her?

6. How can we maintain her loyalty to our brand? (Hint: It starts with getting all of the above right.)

WHAT WOMEN WANT

The blind spots in your business are often things you haven't even thought matter to women, yet they do.

Take my recent car purchase. For six months of 2016 I had been in the market, visiting car dealerships, speaking to the sales team, ready and willing then and there to buy a new car. But I could not get the sales attention I wanted and needed. People looked at me as though I wasn't serious, and failed to call me back. One even asked if my husband was involved in this decision.

Months came and went. I dropped in and out of dealerships and still no-one converted my sale. It was not until I went to a Volvo dealership on a quiet sales day (New Year's Eve) that a young woman approached me and started up the right kind of conversation. What did I drive?

What was I looking for? How long had I been looking? She was not even from sales — she worked in the after-sales team. But she sensed my frustration so she implored her buddy, the salesman, to help me into my next car. That day I purchased, not because of the salesman, but because of female empathy.

In her book *Eveolution*,[5] Faith Popcorn shares a truth about women: 'If she has to ask it's too late.' What this means for business is that women really won't accept being invisible to your brand, as I felt I was to so many automotive companies.

Your business must anticipate her needs, meet her expectations and deliver her desired outcomes.

You must 'get' her, not just in the way your product delivers physically, financially and symbolically, but also in the way you communicate all of this with her.

More than anything, you need to understand ways in which you can simplify her life. Bring back pump service in petrol stations, streamline your buying and selling process, introduce online commerce, deliver to her desk or door, and consider her time when booking appointments at your clinic, salon or consultation. Sell convenience in sizes, understand women are all shapes and sizes, size up the competition and go that step further to connect to women.

Whatever it is you do, whatever industry you are in, you need to make the process easy. The product must be better and add value, NOT time, to her life.

A FRESH TAKE ON FOOD

After blitzing the book market, Amazon has set its sights on fresh food. The company has revolutionised the way we shop; and guess who is their ideal target audience?

Busy women, who still predominantly buy the groceries, need the convenience of delivered groceries and consumer goods more than anyone. Now they can get it from AmazonFresh, a US grocery delivery service, and the integrated Amazon Dash, a voice-operated device that can be used to order goods over the internet.

The Amazon Dash technology allows you say the name of any product you have run low on at home, or to scan its barcode, and build up a digital shopping list that can be used to order from AmazonFresh.

Then there is Amazon Go, a specifically designed store that, at the time I'm writing this, is being trialled in the United States. Shoppers scan their smartphone as they enter the store and anything you put into your bag or trolley will be automatically charged to your account as you leave. No checkout queue — all you do is walk out of the shop.

These options don't just provide ease and convenience; they offer a whole new way of engaging with time-poor women who are always on the go.

ROLE REVITALISED

In the movie *I Don't Know How She Does It*, there is a scene where the lead character, finance executive Kate Reddy, is wide awake in the middle of the night while her family sleep soundly around her. She muses on the statistics that show women with children sleep less at night because they are too busy thinking about all the things they have to do the next day. She writes her to-do list on the bedroom wall, including everything from a client meeting the next day to taking the kids to school to finding more couple time with her husband to arranging food for the kindergarten bake sale the next week.

This is not just the script of a Hollywood movie. It is the real-life experience of many women today. Any business looking to form a relationship with a female customer has to take into account the many roles she juggles (see figure 4.1), and embrace the fact that she could be wearing any one of many hats at the time she's interacting with you.

Figure 4.1: the many roles of modern women

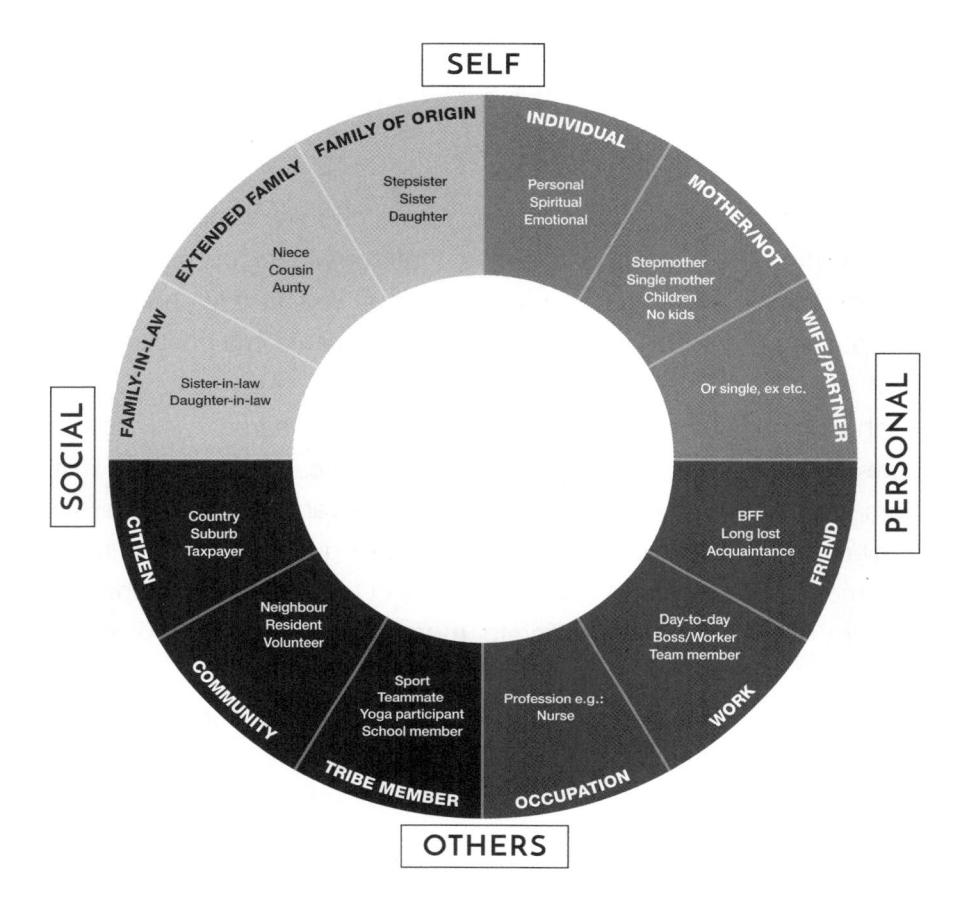

She may be out buying her husband a new shirt before swinging past the school to pick up her child. She may be flying to another city or state for a meeting while managing multiple phone calls with her executive assistant or friends. Then there's the online grocery shopping to do before she heads home to cook dinner.

Some days she may operate mostly in the role of mother or partner, whereas on a weekend she may spend more time in the community or entertaining friends.

At all times the modern woman has to switch roles nimbly and with skill. Being so busy can add to feelings that overwhelm and stress. This is something you need to be acutely aware of! You have to understand this paradigm and find ways to contribute to her life in a positive way.

Each woman is a unique individual with her own character strengths, flaws and idiosyncrasies. The one-dimensional caricature of 'the little homemaker' from the 1950s is no longer relevant. To portray her as in awe of a discounted supermarket item, or gushing at the efficacy of a mop, or happily whiling away her day in the bathroom, kitchen or laundry, raises an instant red flag for modern and enlightened women.

You need to wake up and acknowledge that the modern woman is much more multifaceted than this if you want to have any sort of long-term relationship with her, which is what we'll look at next.

Confronting and washing away the stains of past generations of chauvinism and bias was what Ariel washing powder did in India in its 2016 breakthrough communication cleverly hashtagged #sharetheload. The ad was a runaway success and soon went viral on YouTube.

The ad begins with a modern Indian mum arriving home from work to her family including her father, son and husband. Without pausing, she commences her domestic role while her husband relaxes on the couch watching television. Meanwhile she takes a work call, fetches tea, cooks dinner and puts on a load of washing while her son plays underfoot. Her father, the narrator, sits at the kitchen table observing this juggling act ruefully.

It is a moment of epiphany for him, and he begins to compose a letter of apology, in which he pledges to take responsibility for housework in his own home. At the end we see him arrive back in his own home where, to his wife's confusion, he insists on doing his own washing in order to #sharetheload.

Every father already #sharingtheload will feel a sense of satisfaction, but those who aren't cannot fail to notice the disparity and feel a tiny prick of conscience. Ariel smartly captured audience attention by showing empathy with women. In any marketer's book, this shows just how compelling the right 'marketing-to-women' campaign can be.

The bottom line is that Ariel showed an honest and insightful understanding of a modern woman's world — a world that includes both career and family. None of the usual computer-animated graphics or scientific proof, no red wine or grass stains, no happy housewife admiring her washing machine!

By creating empathy and emotion that truly connects to their female audience, Ariel demonstrated that they actually understand women's need to be seen and connected to.

Josy Paul, chairman and chief creative officer for the agency BBDO India, commented on the stunning success of 'Share the Load': 'It isn't a baseline or a campaign, it is an invitation to men. The feedback and emotional responses sustain you, you wonder why you haven't done this before. We created a movement and it was a success.'

India's P&G Ariel brand campaign, Share The Load, disrupted its category through a creative refocus on the contribution of women in a paternalist society. It has won top awards, and it doubled its value and sales by 106 per cent and 105 per cent respectively.

CHAPTER 5

ARE WE DATING OR IN A RELATIONSHIP?

A divorced guy I know had me enthralled during a conversation about the end of his marriage. He said the veritable straw that broke the relationship's back was 'the dirty plates left on the bench instead of stacked in the dishwasher'. His wife went from politely reminding to eventually nagging him — until finally she just packed up and left it all behind.

Sounds like a common scenario, right? The kind we see in TV comedy sketches or hear from friends at weekend barbecues.

This guy really believed that his marriage ended because of a bunch of dirty dishes he overlooked one too many times. But was it really down to this detail or might it have been that she quite simply got tired of being 'invisible'? The guy wore blinkers that stopped him from seeing the full picture, so eventually she stopped talking and left his field of vision entirely.

There is a lesson in this for us all, including those of us in the business and commercial world. A woman wants to be heard, loved, respected and understood. She wants to know that the relationship is working for both of you. She is keeping up her end of the contract — she chose to buy into you in the first place, and she remains loyal through repeat purchase. She is your fan and talks to everyone about you in the most positive light. At the same time, she too loves to be recognised and rewarded and seen in a positive light. So she expects reciprocal behaviour from you.

Nothing annoys me more than the way Australian groceries and FMCG products are sold using women depicted either as brainless fools delighted by price discounts brought to them by inane singing minstrels, or as helpless victims of germs found lurking invisibly in their bathrooms.

If you ignore a woman's relationship with your brand then you are effectively blind to her needs and one day she will pack her bags and leave.

LONG-LASTING CONSUMER LOVE

If you are not actively looking to improve your relationship with your female audience by listening to her needs, then you are taking for granted your relationship with your main customer — the person spending her money with your business.

In order to deal with all the stuff she has to think about, the modern woman maintains an ongoing relationship assessment scorecard for all the businesses and brands she juggles throughout her life. As chief purchasing officer of her home, she uses an intuitive and easily accessed system to classify the hundreds of things entering her home, head and heart.

Her scorecard has a column for hits and a column for misses. The hits are big red ticks, smiley-face emojis, gold stars; the misses are big, bold, angry black crosses. And she keeps a mental tally of these, so as soon as you have more crosses than ticks you are moved to her list of brands that need to be replaced by a more empathetic alternative.

The place a
brand wants to aim to be,
of course, is close to her heart, up
on the positive side of the scorecard.
Faced with the constant competing
priorities of her busy professional and
personal life, she is more likely to spend
money with the business that makes itself
visible and relevant to her world: 'We see
you, and we bring something you need to the
relationship we share.'

A classic example of this is athletic sports
powerhouse Nike. Despite leading the
charge through the 1970s and 1980s
to embrace women's growing
engagement with personal fitness,
not to mention sponsorship
and support of great female
Olympic athletes, Nike still
needed to find their true
'goddess' power. It was not
until the early 2000s that
they started to look deeper
into women's attitudes and
feelings and the 'emotional'
worlds of females.[1]

Nike threw away what they knew
about traditional perceptions of
sport (as seen through a male lens)
and started with a clean slate,
building from the ground up with
a whole new concentrated
focus on their female
customer.

After 30 years of
making shoes for athletes,
they finally took a mould of a real
woman's foot. And they discovered
that women's feet weren't just generally
smaller than men's but were also shaped
differently — and in some areas were actually
bigger. Nike held on to the attributes women
still expected of Nike — the performance, the
tech and the tough factors — but built on these
to find ways of resonating with women, visually,
emotionally and functionally.

The move paid off. Through the late 2000s
and subsequent decade Nike has grown its
business and gained more female market
share. The women's line gave them
$2 billion positive revenue and the
company predicted that by 2020
the women's market would gen-
erate $11 billion, a faster growth
rate than the men's market.[2]

This is a great example of the
two different-but-equal lenses
at work. Nike showed that they
could hold on to the valuable DNA
that defined their success but move
with the times and embrace the new
worldview of women. Their willingness
to adapt to the needs of 50 per cent of
the world and build a new avenue of
revenue has been validated and their
perspective has been adjusted to
better service the true needs
of the female market.

WILL YOU MARRY ME?

We've all been in love at one time or another. Most of us have been through the dizzy infatuation stage or at least have observed this behaviour in others. A customer's journey with your brand and business is similar to any other relationship in terms of the commitment it can take.

Imagine this scenario: A woman and your brand meet, you might have an interaction or two, then you inch along the continuum until you are regularly dating or swapping transactions. A relationship starts to form.

You start to feel something more towards each other. An emotional bond forms. She starts to talk about you to her friends. You feel giddy and excited by all this money she is spending on you. She's taking you to places you've never been. All the time. And your sales are growing, bulging in fact. (Which makes your boss very happy too.)

You want to know you occupy a special place in her heart, that she sees you more than anyone else and is willing to commit to you.

Eventually you want to know you are the only one in her house, head and heart in a solid relationship that will stand the test of time.

All relationships with businesses have feelings attached to them, whether we realise it or not. They may at first come across as purely transactional, but much more is happening on a subconscious level, especially when it comes to female consumers!

For example, when I purchase fuel for my car, I feel as if I am transacting with the business that helps me to complete my journey from point A to point B. The relationship is of low importance to me. The environment can feel 'fuelled' (pun intended) with danger of some kind, with warning signs everywhere, pump anxiety about the kind of fuel you are using, people coming and going, the driver behind you waiting impatiently for you to leave. You take your kids into the shop, where the person at the register is distracted by multitasking.

For my nearly hundred-dollar spend, it's usually not a great experience. At a deeper level of cognitive thought, I register either a positive or a negative feeling. There are at least three service stations I choose not to go to because of the negative feelings I have when I am there. It may be they are too big and busy, if I have little kids with me. I often have to wait a long time in the queue. Or they are unfriendly, with not a smile or pleasant exchange to be had. So I wait to go to the one that's just the right size, with friendly staff and a car wash for those busy weeks when I can't find an alternative.

So if an oil company wanted to attract me to their brand, to persuade me to drive the extra distance to spend my hundred dollars at their pump, they would need to engage me on a much deeper level.

Figure 5.1 (overleaf) outlines the journey a woman takes, from ignoring you to loving your brand.

Figure 5.1: female brand-love relationship — a value model

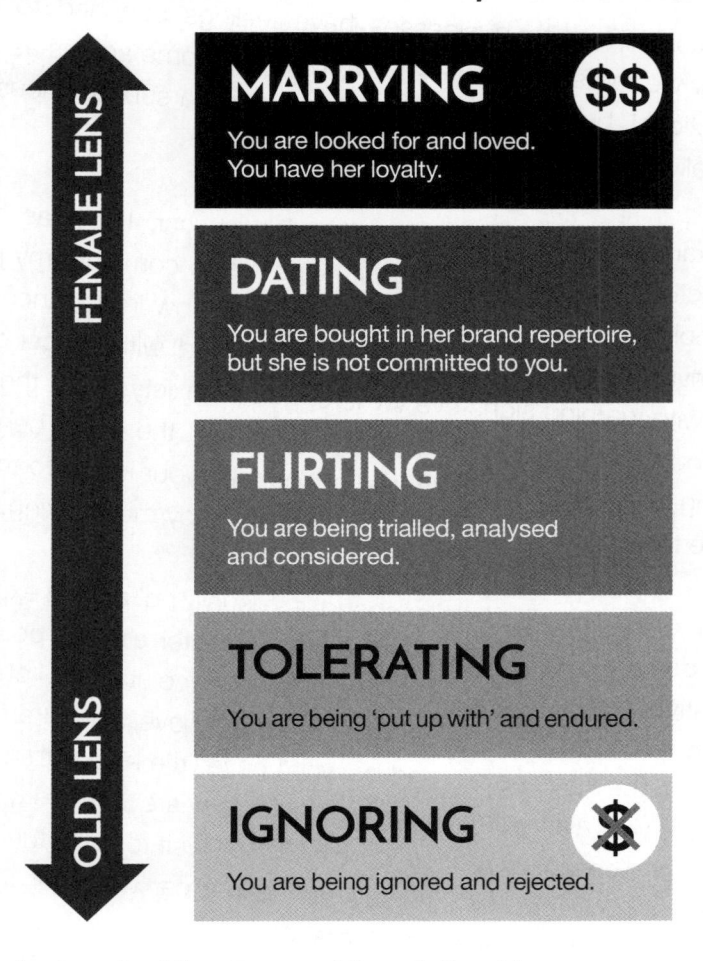

Let's look at each of the stages of the relationship.

FROM IGNORING YOU TO MARRYING YOU

Every customer relationship you have with a female will take place somewhere along the continuum illustrated in figure 5.1. So where do you think you are at? And, more importantly, what do you do to keep your relationship moving up the ladder to something more secure and long-lasting?

WHEN SHE IS <u>IGNORING</u> YOU

At this stage you are probably completely invisible to her. You've not made an effort to identify her, get to know her or become relevant in her life. You have not met the standards she expects from you and she has already made a decision not to pursue a relationship with you. She uses her blinkers to filter you from her really busy world.

If she is ignoring your business you likely have a heavily male-dominated business and brand culture and are oblivious to the needs of women. You're failing to resonate with her on a rational product level and definitely in the emotional brand space. Even if you are selling a women's product or operating in the female audience space, this may be the thing that stops lots of women from choosing you at all!

If you are a big global company, then perhaps you haven't even thought that you need to engage more women directly to ensure you remain profitable. As she is invisible to you, you are missing out on seeing her true value. You may be safe until someone else enters your market and turns it upside down. Think what Uber did to the taxi industry or Airbnb to hotels, and what Amazon is doing to the grocery sector.

You are suffering from an identity crisis, in part because you are a culture that believes in rotating through many different stakeholders or brand custodians. The average tenure for brand managers and marketers is under 24 months, so it is likely your brand changes its 'personality' according to who is in the chair. This constant vacillation makes you appear to be unreliable, unpredictable and difficult to understand. Women can't relate to you, and every time she thinks she has worked out who you are, and contemplates talking to you, you produce another personality.

IGNORING TOUGH TALK

Get gender-smart.
When we are looking at a business or brand through a traditional/male lens, we are very likely acting on principles that hark back to a different era and a pre-enlightened state of consciousness.

Adopt new marketing tools.
Marketing principles were developed over time from a very masculine worldview, appropriate for a stage of social development when men were breadwinners and women were homemakers.

Open your eyes to the female prescription.
Most women are financially managing not only their own income but also the household income (75 per cent of the discretionary spend by 2028).

Make an effort to future proof.
With projections that more women will enter the workforce, and will be paid equally in the coming decades, it's an investment with long-term value.

WHEN SHE IS
<u>TOLERATING</u> YOU

In her world, she is tolerating you because you may be the only option available to her and she has found no other convenient alternatives—yet. She's patient and will give you a go, until one day something irresistible happens. Will you survive it?

You are meeting her needs on one level, but she'd never actually admit she's in a relationship with you. In fact, she avoids talking about you.

To put it bluntly, you're a 'place-holder' only until something better comes along.

Something about you turns her off. You might have a great product but crummy packaging or incompetent sales staff or a gratingly annoying advertising campaign that makes her turn the radio off.

You are not giving her value for money. You are priced too high for her expectations and the value equation in her head. You can get away with this pricing until a competitor comes along and offers her a better return on investment. Think of how Ikea, Asos and Virgin disrupted their markets.

You haven't changed or evolved with the times. New players have come in, and while you were taking her for granted, someone new started engaging her in a conversation and really noticing that you'd been neglecting her needs.

You got complacent. You won her love with a great campaign or product improvement a few years ago but haven't delighted her since. She's wondering if this is all there is in your future together. She's tried changing her attitude to you, but she has brought all she can to this relationship and she's starting to wonder what else is out there.

TOLERATING TOUGH TALK

Start a conversation.

Most people will have been in this relationship phase. It's the stage when one person is willing to overlook some of the less attractive qualities of the other, for now. Either you will learn you need to make some changes, and start engaging with her, or she will find a better match elsewhere.

Ask how things might improve.

Women are hardwired to create harmony around their campfire, and they are constantly looking for ways to improve their world. This inbuilt preference means she is always looking for ways to make her immediate environment a better place, so just ask her what she needs.

Act—now!

It's not too late to change. She wants you to understand her perspective and is willing to give you the feedback and help to smooth off those rough edges. But don't make her wait too long. It's these little things that are like the dirty dishes in the sink. If she has to put up with these things for too long, she's going to give up and leave.

WHEN SHE IS <u>FLIRTING</u> WITH YOU

All in all, you tick enough boxes for her to form some sort of relationship with you, but she needs to know more about you before she'll take things a step further. You look good, but what's underneath that charming surface?

She has started the process of researching, comparing you with your competitors, and has put you on the short list for a potential long-term relationship. She mentioned you to a friend or group and the response she got was positive, so you passed round one, but will you make it through the next one?

You are offering her the right product and price, and thanks to your smart media placement she's noticing you more and more in her world. You are now in her field of vision, maybe on her social media feed or on the shows she watches on catch-up TV. Somehow you have made it onto her radar and she has decided not to 'block' you.

But there are others out there and many of them are a lot like you. What makes you different and more interesting? How do you stand out in the crowd and make her knees go weak and set her heart fluttering? How do you really secure her interest?

FLIRTING TOUGH TALK

Be reliable.
The opportunity to get to know each other better is yours to keep and yours to lose. She has given you a chance and now is your time to deliver.

Remain consistent.
You get great feedback and a positive response to your brand. She notices your hard work and it's paying off. But don't rest on your laurels. The exchanges are as yet only small and are still fresh.

Build trust.
You can't go changing now. She's only just bought into the vision you have promised. If she thinks you were only faking it to win her attention, you won't get a second chance. Be warned!

You look the part. Her ideal and your brand image are aligned. Everything about you is stacking up. You are worth her time and investment, and she is getting something positive back when she interacts with you.

You are talking her language—whether it's the copy on the packaging or social media or your PR campaign—she has noticed you and is picking up what you are putting down. She has bought in.

It's a form of 'femvertising', creating empathy with her by caring about what she cares about. You are pro-women, and this is a big deal for her in a world that hasn't been having much empathy or intimacy with her until now.

A review of your market has revealed that women are a big part of it. Now you have begun to see women through the new filter and to deliver a better experience with your brand. You have listened and learned—and are producing new products to meet her needs.

Your company is embracing a new gender focus for all staff, to create gender awareness internally and externally. For this, women are starting to love you and include you in their communities.

DATING TOUGH TALK

Be consistent.

You might see a sales spike and feel really confident. The work you have done has paid off—you have won her over... but this is no time to rest. Your relationship is only beginning and your long-term commitment is yet to be proved.

Put in the effort.

In this phase she is working out if you will be the brand she loves above all others, so a bit of romance will keep her enthralled. She needs to know you are serious about her.

Watch every move.

What you do will make or break the relationship, so keep your eyes and ears open, and get ready to make a move that will secure her hand in marriage.

WHEN SHE IS <u>MARRYING</u> YOU

You have consistently been there for her and she loves your dependability in her life. You've made it really obvious you care about the relationship and you have responded to her when she's been unhappy.

She tried others and you were simply the best. You deliver on all her brand expectations and have found the right value equation that makes her want to stay loyal to you.

Your relationship is symbiotic. You continue to meet her needs and she continues to be there for you. You've engaged her in social forums and have a closed group of 'VIPs' who enjoy a close relationship with the brand custodians at head office.

You continue to surprise, delight and reward her with unexpected gifts and 'flowers' for no reason other than that you are invested in the relationship.

Constantly improving service levels, keeping up with time-saving technology, and providing customer service with empathy, connection and understanding are key. Remember that it is important to reinvent yourself and not just become an older, greyer version of your glory days. Adapting with fashions, trends and innovations is the essence of staying relevant to modern woman.

MARRYING TOUGH TALK

Keep it up.
You are on the road to becoming a market leader. You are becoming increasingly profitable and enjoying the improved revenue and augmented share value. The investment has been worthwhile. The hard work is paying off. Just don't take it for granted!

Reinvent often.
You are innovating constantly, launching new versions, announcing breakthroughs and showing her that you are actively listening and responding. Your relationship continues to flourish. Do research to make sure you are on the pulse with her needs at all times. Keep 'talking it through'.

Are you getting your relationship right?

What steps will you take to ensure you are where you want to be?

BUT WHAT ABOUT HIM?

When I met my husband, he lived in the proverbial bachelor pad. The first time I was going to see where he lived was on a Valentine's Day date. Instead of inspecting the pad, he spontaneously arranged for us to dine and stay at a hotel. Thinking it was another romantic bid after a string of memorable gestures, I was swept off my feet.

It turned out, though, that he was so worried about what I might think of the house he was living in that he was buying time while the house got some serious cleaning attention.

His sensitivity to 'women's standards' was empathetic. His survival instinct kicked in too — he did not want to drive me away by appearing not to share my domestic values. He really thought the state of the bathroom, the build-up of dirty dishes, the unvacuumed floors and his flatmate's 'floor-drobe' would make me think twice about him. So he waited until he could make it look presentable before he let me see it.

It was probably a smart move — but the truth is I would have found an excuse for his unkempt house because there were enough other cues that told me he cared about cleanliness: his clothes, grooming and spotless car told me much about his character. I would have assumed the mess belonged to his housemate!

The point is we all allow some leeway in our relationships — even those we have with brands. But women won't tolerate it if their values are undermined for too long.

My husband says I make the house we live in with our two daughters 'a home'. Left to him, he says, it would not have nearly the amount of throw cushions, soft furnishings, living plants and attention to detail that my female nesting instinct brings to our shared space.

When you understand and meet the needs of women you make the men happy by default.

While men may not seek it actively, they will appreciate when a business makes an effort to improve its offering and delight women.

Is it because females do more consuming? And are we socialised into these gender roles or are women hardwired to see things differently?

It is probably a combination of all three. It is generally accepted that if you meet the needs and expectations of a woman, you will exceed a man's.

A DOUBLE RACE

One of my clients, a racing club for the prestigious Cox Plate, was losing market share. Over the years the venue had become the last bastion of the male punter. While rival courses had attracted massive crowds of women and men who loved the gentrification of horse racing and the tradition of dressing up and wearing hats, attendance at Moonee Valley was flat.

This course entertained a lot of old blokes wearing tracksuit pants and runners, and the only women to be seen were serving behind the bar.

The business knew there was a new audience with an appetite for racing. So together we launched a season of twilight racing. We knew we needed to rebuild the offering from top to bottom if the crowds were to be persuaded to spend money walking through their gate.

Over the subsequent three months everything was reimagined through a female lens. It was accepted that if we could convince young women to attend, then the young men would want to go along as well.

The brand identity, logos and signage, advertising, collateral and chosen ambassadors were all upgraded, the menu and beverages changed and the bathroom amenities modernised. Sponsors came on board to reflect the new audience expected. The style went from traditional coarsely masculine to modern, stylish and elegant, with visual semiotics that reflected the kinds of clothing, entertainment and brands that the women and girls attending coveted.

A few weeks after the campaign was launched, the first night brought a 33 per cent increase in gate sales. This success continued over the season. It was the best financial period the club had enjoyed in decades, with more people (especially women) attending the marquee Cox Plate event than ever before.

DON'T PINK AND SHRINK

Women are tougher critics than men when it comes to their expectations and experiences with brands. In fact, they are a tougher and more critical audience in general. For example, Spike Cramphorn's 'Gender effects in advertising' study[3] demonstrated that women are 'more engaged consumers' than their male counterparts.

Conversely, a business that takes something traditionally masculine and merely 'makes it pink and makes it shrink' will not fool women into a relationship, because it does not authentically meet their hopes and dreams. It has applied some superficial understanding of women based on a clumsy masculine premise, but it has not been reimagined through a female lens.

'Pink and shrink' is a classic example of where business goes wrong when attempting to engage with women. In the next chapter, we'll bust the other big business myths you might be getting all wrong.

RICH LOVE

When you get it right you can expect:

1 greater revenue through more sales and repeat business

an increase in average spend and frequency of purchase **2**

3 reduced marketing waste and increased ROI

better brand advocacy and loyalty

organic growth in audience through positive word of mouth

breakthrough profits in a stagnant or sluggish market

focused innovations and brand extension

CHAPTER 6

BUSTING THE BIGGEST BUSINESS MYTHS

Back in the 1980s, I went to a new school that had until that year been an all-boys school. When the new co-ed campus welcomed girls, the school's enrolment numbers pretty much doubled.

For the new girls, it was exciting as well as confusing. We were outnumbered and were something of a spectacle to the boys, who had previously only had to compete with other boys.

Even as a ten-year-old, it occurred to me that apart from the uniform, which had been thoughtfully styled by a fashion designer, there was no sign of a female lens there at all.

The curriculum was essentially unchanged, including all the masculine textbooks — views of history, war and male war heroes — that were designed from a male perspective around the message that 'anything was possible' if you fought hard for it. Palpably missing were female role models and stories about women climbing metaphorical mountains.

During weekly school assemblies we listened to stories from the Bible (God and Jesus and all those male disciples), the headmaster's sermon, and of course the school sports updates. We may not have even been allowed to play the games, but we still had to endure these regular reports on the boys' on-field prowess. One of the greatest honours for a Grammarian was the opportunity to be drafted into the first XI to play cricket at Lord's in London. There was no equivalent prize for a girl to aspire to.

Honour boards were instead laden with boys' sports and boys' names, the walls hung with oil paintings of past male principals. It was a monoculture that had decades of catching up to do to become relevant and inspiring for the girls. We needed to feel we had a place in the heart of the school that was not watching from the sidelines or just an afterthought.

This unconscious gender conditioning continues to play out in our education system, at school and university, and to shape the workplace.

Our early exposure sets up the patterns we carry into adulthood and our careers. So when we look at business and the workforce now, it's clear that the solution is not just to throw males and females in together without any thought for how they are different. Instead we need to engage each of them in ways that best suit their individual needs.

There's this notion of 'technical debt' in a start-up company, where you wing it and are scrappy for a while, but if you don't come back and clean up your code then you eventually pay the price. We also need to be aware of 'diversity debt' in this way.

This is particularly true in the tech industry, where diversity debt starts very early in the process. From childhood, boys are encouraged to do the technical classes, then the girls see only the boys doing these classes and think it's not for them. Early on they are pushed out of the tech industry.

We recently visited a school that was struggling with a lack of girls in their engineering classes. In years 7 and 8, when the classes were compulsory, the girls would frequently hold the top marks in the class. But in Year 9, when the classes were electives, there were zero girls opting in. Why?

We were asked to look at the curriculum and make it more appealing to girls (which we did). When we got stuck into discussing how the program would be rolled out, we realised the problem wasn't the classes, it was the way the girls' classes were marketed and the process the girls were given to select the classes.

There was a school expo with stands about each class that had no women on the stands, only men. 'Do you hand out flyers?' I asked. 'Yes!' they excitedly declared as they handed over a flyer with a Meccano car and a game controller on the front. I opened the flyer to find pictures of students who were ALL boys. 'We just wanted to show students in the flyer' was the logic behind it.

The more we feature boys as 'what tech looks like', the more it will become what tech looks like. We need to intervene and create marketing that reflects not just how things are, but what results we wish to see if we have any hope of creating an inclusive environment for women and girls in technology careers.

```html
<!DOCTYPE html>
<html>
<head>
<title>Get your geek on</title>
</head>
<body>
</body>
</html>
```

WHERE ARE WE GOING WRONG?

Not long ago I asked a chief marketing officer at a telco service provider what the gender breakdown of her customers was. Her eyes rolled at me, like I'd asked her something that wasn't at all relevant. She assumed that the market, like the population, would be around 50/50. In a nutshell, she hadn't even thought about it.

Why is it that when we see the word 'gender' in the context of 'business' our insides feel tight and we run for the hills?

If you're currently rejecting the relevance of gender in your business (see chapter 1), then it's likely you most identify with this feeling. It's also likely you feel this way because you believe in one of the following Five Business Myths:

1. **I have an all-female team — I get it.**

2. **We're equal opportunity — tick.**

3. **We've got a person to tackle this.**

4. **My budget isn't big enough.**

5. **We've done femvertising. Job done.**

Well I'm about to burst your bubble! Let's explore each myth in detail.

MYTH 1

I HAVE AN ALL-FEMALE TEAM — I GET IT.

At a conference once, I was having a discussion with an extremely clever CEO who had been running his petcare start-up for a decade. Only now new players were starting to steal market share and he was being forced to compete on price.

We talked about his customers and how he might make them more loyal and stop them switching brands. Deeper probing revealed that 80 per cent of his customers were women, yet he had not thought to focus on the gender of his customers to understand their behaviour, average spend and purchasing cycles.

As I talked about the merits of segmenting by gender, he told me something I hear all the time when discussing this issue with business: 'My staff are nearly all women, so they already know how to sell to women.'

The truth is, having a nearly all-female team does not make you or them experts on engaging your female clients or customers.

Having the same genitals as your audience does not make you an expert at understanding, marketing and selling to them. Women have grown up learning the same principles of marketing and reading from the same playbooks as men. The majority of our management books have been written by the guys: Napoleon Hill, Warren Buffett, Seth Godin, Simon Sinek, Charles Drucker, Stephen Covey. It's all sage advice but it's all seen through a male lens.

Leaders who maintain that their business is already doing a good job of catering to and effectively engaging with the female economy, simply because they have women in senior marketing roles or a team made up mostly of women, need to see if the maths add up.

What does your data say? Are you really doing a good job of engaging your female audience?

Assumptions like this are dangerous. It reminds me of a colleague I once worked with. Born in London to a Chinese father and an English mother, people mistook her for a native Chinese She knew little of the culture and spoke not a word of Cantonese, Mandarin or any other Chinese dialect. Merely because of her appearance, everyone assumed she would be the expert on all things Asian. Wrong!

Expertise on how to run a successful business comes from deep study and familiarity, as well as meeting the unmet needs of the market and therefore creating a profitable and enduring relationship.

Over the past six decades of progress on legal and ethical standards, along with workplace policies and initiatives, we have seen amazing social change and recognition of women's rights. Yet this has brought much confusion to the world of business.

Sexism. Discrimination. Equality. Feminism. These words ignite fear in many. The conversation is a minefield that many business execs avoid entering for fear of making a wrong move. No company wants to be accused of discrimination or of opposing 'equal opportunity'. But this is the fly in the ointment.

It is wishful thinking to expect that internal solutions such as making 'Diversity and Inclusion' a part of staff training and tasking the HR department with stamping out unconscious bias can ensure deeper engagement with your customer and consumers — the women who are outside of your business.

Segmenting male and female markets is not discrimination; actually it is the opposite. It is about being more sensitive to each gender through a concerted effort to understand them better.

There is a fundamental flaw that occurred along the journey of women who wanted to be considered as 'different but equal' to men. It's a misaligned view of what gender equality ought be.

True equality does not mean women are treated in precisely the same way as men. It means that women have a range of opportunity equivalent to men's but that this opportunity takes a form that is appropriate for them.

This includes an expectation that their needs are recognised and realised. Businesses that understand this and focus their lens on the customer who makes the consumer decisions will win their dollars.

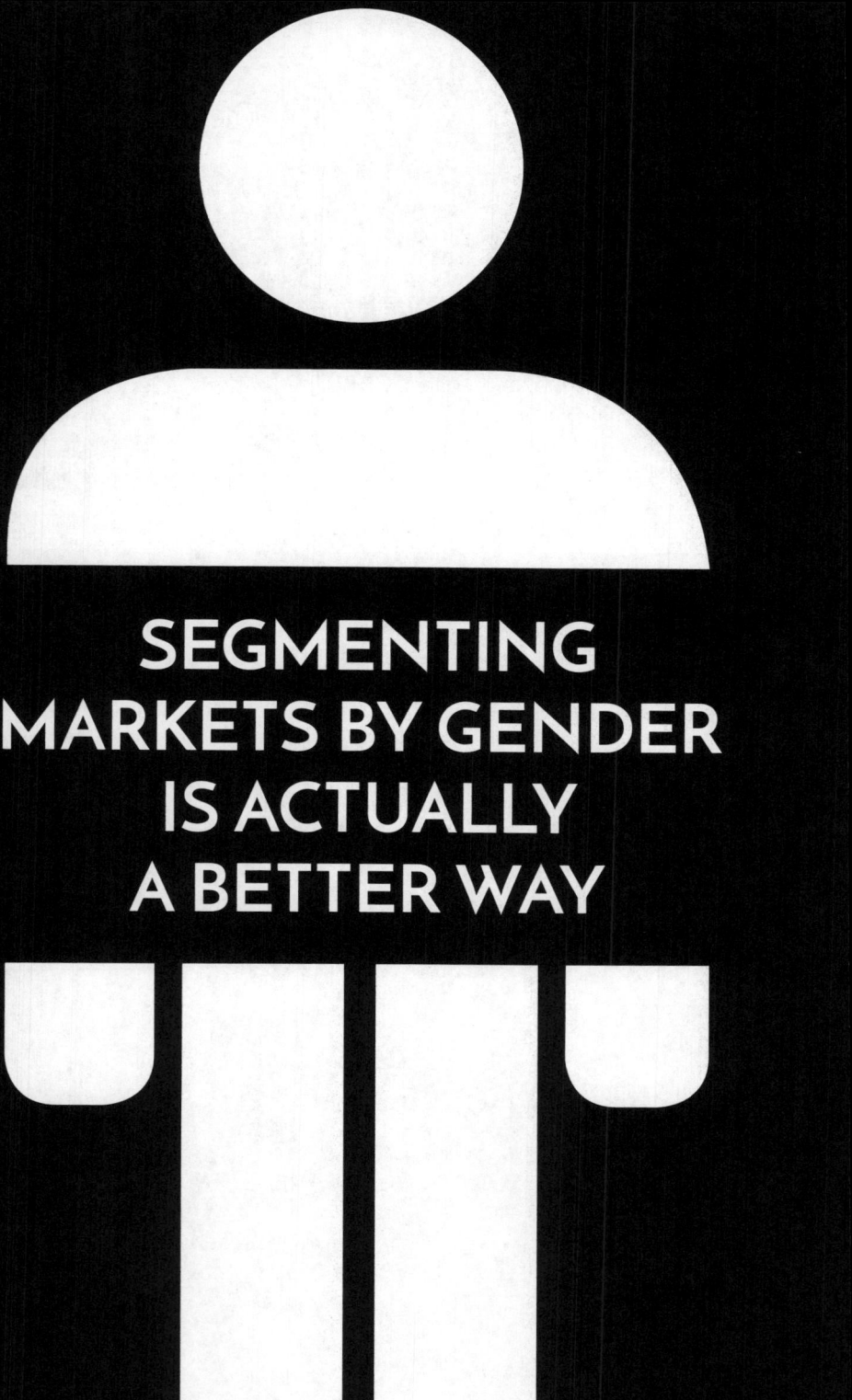

SEGMENTING
MARKETS BY GENDER
IS ACTUALLY
A BETTER WAY

TO CONNECT TO YOUR AUDIENCE SUCCESSFULLY AND AUTHENTICALLY.

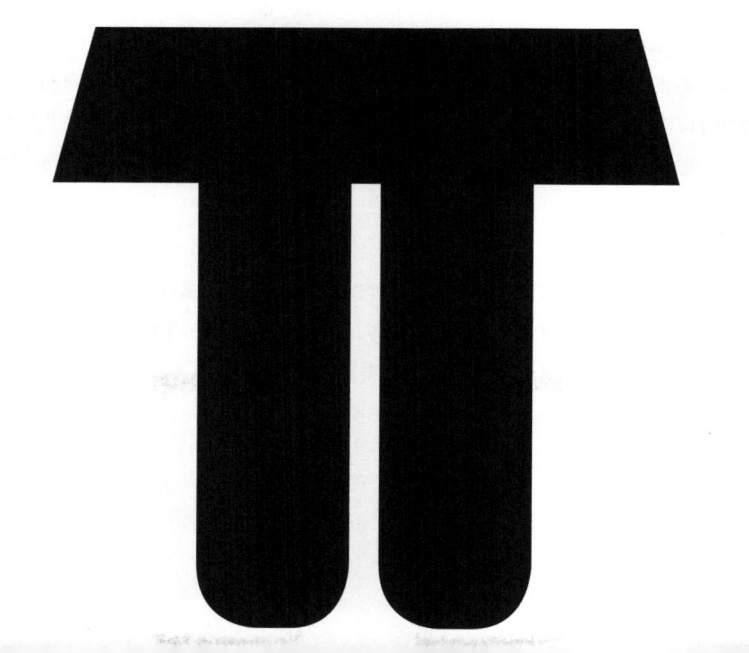

MYTH 3

WE'VE GOT A PERSON TO TACKLE THIS.

I have seen some businesses attempt to transform their organisation to attract more women by hiring for the role of 'female engagement officer'. This reminds me of when former Australian prime minister Tony Abbott headed up the 'Office for Women', and nothing changed.[1]

Creating a role on the org chart with a token title is delusional. Unless the entire organisation is given top-down support from management, and there is an explicit move from within the business to create a female business culture that seeks to understand the needs of its consumers and clients, then creating such a position is wishful thinking.

As the consultants from McKinsey, EY and Catalyst remind us, including more women across the business is a start to getting more profitable. But even more important is a shift from a culture fundamentally shaped by the male lens to one that allows all staff to see through both male and female lenses.

This is a constant, ongoing conversation, and perhaps a way to think about structuring teams in such a way that neither lens starts to impair the visibility of the other. We don't want to favour one way of seeing and thinking and, in doing so, weaken the other.

MYTH 4

MY BUDGET ISN'T BIG ENOUGH.

To develop insights in business that lead to actual market advantage, looking at gender differences is essential. We've spent time looking at how the very obvious behavioural and socially conditioned disparities between men and women can be used to commercial advantage.

Often, though, even the thought of this work leaves the C-suite, marketers and SME business owners in a cold sweat. Their first reaction is that their budget could not possibly stretch across the two gender markets: different products, different distribution, communications — how would that work? Would they be diluting their funds by 50 per cent?

The short answer is no.

You can't treat your female audience like an 'emerging market' and apportion a small budget. If women make up, say, 80 per cent of your market, then that is how much you need to spend to focus more on them.

Womenomics starts with financially modelling the gender segments. How much are male and female customers worth? Average transaction and cost per acquisition? Value over a lifetime? Size of potential market within the competitive set?

With the sophisticated granularity of these financial audits, targeting males and females means you can now be sure you are getting bang for every buck your business spends.

Even better news is that getting it right for women has a halo effect on your brand for men. Because women generally have higher expectations of businesses and brands, meeting their demands invariably means men are more satisfied too. If your audience is still gender-neutral, use of the female lens to rework the brand will ensure that you haven't alienated the guys.

Creating deeper relationships with women results in less manufacturing and marketing waste and much greater ROI.

MYTH 5

WE'VE DONE FEMVERTISING. JOB DONE.

Femvertising usually looks like this: you find an issue that women feel passionate about (such as their desire to be treated equally), attach your brand to their cause and promote the message to the world with a #hashtag. Right?

Wrong.

The case for this kind of real and emotionally stirring messaging is strong. It has shown us that messages in the media have the power to change perceptions, but it must be real and deep and authentic throughout the business. You can't paint over a male-lensed culture with a wave of pink glitter. If this is as far as the female lens can see, then it's really only lip service.

For example, a bank that talks about being pro-women by advocating for equality and creating more wealth for them, but has no proactive wealth strategies in its own business, or pays women less than men throughout its own organisation, could be seen as disingenuous.

Remember the case study of Unilever in chapter 3? There was a contradiction between their pro–modern women brand Dove and their pro–macho men brand Lynx, which frequently used 'dumb and gorgeous' stereotypes of female models in a hyper-sexualised way. Fortunately, the company woke up and vowed to ditch the outdated, hypocritical and inconsistent messaging.

CASE STUDY
BLACK GIRL MAGIC

Marley Dias

In 2015 an 11-year-old schoolgirl in the United States named Marley Dias complained to her mother about her school reading materials, in which all the narratives were about white boys and their dogs.[2] So her mother challenged her thinking by asking, 'What are you going to do about it?'

She started a book drive calling for more books with black girl protagonists that she could relate to, using the hashtag #blackgirlmagic and #1000BlackGirlBooks.

This story is a wake-up call for every business leader, and indeed anyone, who finds themselves stopped in their tracks by old-school or male-lensed unconscious bias. There *is* something you can do to change the tradition. To provide the impetus to look for new solutions, first you need to ask yourself the same question Marley's mum asked her: 'What are you going to do about it?'

The leadership team and the HR department need to examine the unconscious bias within an organisation. But we must also examine our 'external biases' — the ways in which we view, communicate with and treat our customers.

FROM COMA...

A boy and his father are driving home on the freeway from a weekend camping trip when they are involved in a tragic head-on collision. The father dies at the scene of the accident; his son is airlifted to the nearest hospital for life-saving surgery. As they rush the boy into theatre the surgeon looks at him and announces, 'I can't operate on this child, he's my son...'

If you read this riddle and wonder how the young boy can possibly have two fathers, then you'll be with most people. You might assume that the boy has a biological dad and a stepfather. Or maybe the boy didn't know one of his 'fathers', maybe the identity of his real dad was a long-held family secret. Better yet, perhaps the boy has two dads in a gay partnership.

If you assume any of these scenarios, then you assume incorrectly.

Did you ever stop to think that the surgeon is actually the injured child's *mother*?

This is unconscious bias in action. More importantly, it shows how shallow we are when it comes to seeing genders on an equal footing. It explains where the five myths we have just explored come from and why we continue to feed them.

And indeed, it is the reason I chose to use my initials for the front cover of this book. The problem with unconscious bias, of course, is that it happens beneath the surface at a level we are not even aware of or in touch with. That is, until a personal epiphany or a third party exposes the bias to us by holding up a metaphoric mirror and asking us to examine our own behaviour. So that this book had the very best chance of being read by as many people as possible, I cloaked my gender, much as is done in a 'blind résumé'. In doing so, I hoped the arguments in the book would be considered, free of any influence my gender might have on the reader.

In 2016, New Zealand Prime Minister John Key and Wellington mayor Kerry Prendergast took a stand against the times.[3] They replaced the green flashing man on a pedestrian traffic light with a green flashing woman. Token as this act may have been, it was a significant statement from a country that has long supported female-lensed thinking. In fact, New Zealand was the first country to grant women equal political status with the vote.

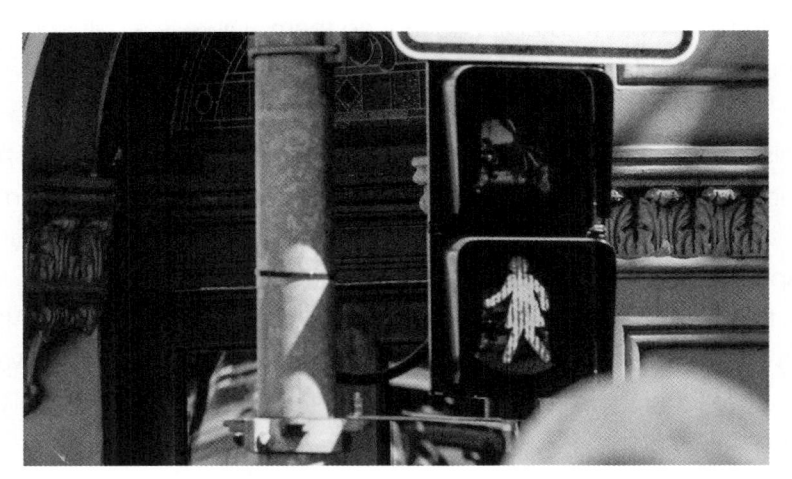

Source: © Ralf Weber

In a small way, this step challenged what we consider 'normal' in society, drawing attention to a very visible example of how unconsciously the male symbol overrules the female.

In the UK, the mayor of London ran with the idea by changing the standard symbol of a man to reflect different representations of gender and sexuality through the familiar gender symbols, sending a message that London was a city that embraced diversity.[4]

In Australia, Melbourne followed suit in 2017 with an initiative from the Committee for Melbourne's Future Focus Group in honour of International Women's Day. Minister for Women Fiona Richardson said the use of a Woman's figure on pedestrian crossings would make public space more inclusive of women. 'There are many small — but symbolically significant — ways that women are excluded from public space ... a culture of sexism is made up of very small issues, like how the default pedestrian crossings use a male figure — and large issues, such as the rate of family violence facing women.'[5]

If you look around your city, you'll see many statues of the men who shaped our society. Plaques adorn the buildings constructed and named after male citizens who built and funded them. There is a palpable lack of recognition of female history even in our physical surroundings.[6]

In history class we learn about our forefathers who explored the world, made the great discoveries, advanced the theories, painted the ceilings, created the art and are represented on our bank notes. In sport today, all-male teams monopolise the weekend papers, and this filters into our water cooler chitchat on Monday morning. It is men who first landed on the moon, commanded the troops in wars, made the iconic speeches — and dominated the news coverage you watched last night.

This is not a blame game, or a hate club against men. It is a simple observation and an invitation to all of us, men and women, to transform.

We are entering an age of enlightenment with a vast range of facts, figures and opportunities available to us to navigate the future. We can mine more data than we have ever before had access to. Businesses can accurately identify audiences and focus on their customers, especially those making the purchasing decisions. This is how you can be confident that you're maximising your business potential.

The male perspective has contributed greatly to the shaping of society, but things need to change if we are to make the most of the opportunities available to forward-thinking businesses today.

... TO CONSCIOUS

Unconscious bias plays a big part in the ongoing blindness that persists in business and society today. The Tropfest film festival of 2017 showed what can happen when all people are judged on merit rather than through a preconceived lens of entitlement or worthiness.[7] For the first time in the festival's history because of the 'blind submission' rule, 50 per cent of women became finalists. Given how men have dominated the winner list in the past, this was an unprecedented development.

Many examples of unconscious bias in the media spring to mind. Australia's biggest supermarkets, because of their large media spend, come up frequently.[8] Each chain features male chefs as ambassadors. They most often create work that features male hero talent and cast, while tending to use women as 'warm props', smiling ornaments exhilarated by the supermarket's offerings but without actually getting a speaking part. This leaves women feeling invisible, unrecognised and, importantly, silenced.

These businesses will face a serious reckoning when competition from Amazon (as noted in chapter 4) carves into their market. Having failed to emotionally connect, recognise and engage women, they have failed to appreciate the value of the main grocery buyer, who should be at the very centre of their business. Instead, the communications and messaging we receive says they see women as incidental characters without a significant voice in their culture.

Then there's the road safety advertisement from TAC in Australia, which created a Neanderthal-like creature, dubbed 'the strongest person', who could withstand the impact of a road collision.[9] But why show only a man, given women also buy, drive and travel in cars? Sure, the figures indicate that young men are most at risk of driving dangerously or irresponsibly, but often young women are in the car with them. This is a glaring example of the unconscious male lens.

Make women more visible — even symbolically, as on pedestrian crossing lights — and we demonstrate the equal partnership the genders should enjoy on this earth. When women are absent from our history, our curriculums, our advertisements and our media, we see a world that views opportunity through only one perspective. And a big blind spot is revealed.

A PERIOD OF TRANSFORMATION

When Facebook moved from being a purely social tool to becoming a business-driven platform for connecting customers and brands, most of my clients either happily accepted this idea or thought up every conceivable reason for why it was a bad idea.

Some buzzed with excitement at the power of bringing their brand into a social space, where co-creation with its real fans in real time would create a community of like-minded souls. They were quick to adopt the idea of a brand becoming 'social' and reaped the benefits by growing early communities that still serve them today.

Others, however, had no sense of affiliation with the platform, typically viewing it as a time-wasting, budget-consuming space where their teenage children hung out. Hanging on to past tradition, they were reflexively closed to the possibility of what could be.

What this highlighted for me was the two very different mindsets of leaders: the growth mindset and the fixed. You can't force someone to do something they don't want to. If their eyes are shut, then the challenge is to open them. They must adapt on their journey along the evolutionary curve to arrive at this new point of development when they are culturally ready.

The same can be said of how we approach gender in business today. The empirical evidence, backed by consistent reports from big consulting companies, tells us we must engage the female economy. Yet, as we see in the model in chapter 1, businesses and leaders are still at very different evolutionary stages in their awareness, acceptance and action.

Monocultures are most likely to fail to capitalise on womenomics. Where a masculine culture dominates, women soon learn to adapt to the groupthink in order to survive. No woman wants to be seen as the squeaky wheel on this issue or to be dubbed the 'feminazi' of the office. Women risk being seen as pushing the 'gender issue' rather than the positive economic growth that will benefit their business.

Essentially, this need to adapt in order to fit in can end up as something akin to Stockholm syndrome, where the victim develops feelings of trust or affection towards their captor as an unconscious means of enduring the situation they are in. Women in the corporate world adapt and even mimic the behaviours of their male counterparts in order to survive in the environment.

I myself have been guilty of writing and creating sexist advertising by acceding to the male lens. When I did write something that empathised with a female perspective, my senior leaders could not relate to it. I was told to scrap the idea and start again.

If your business has a female audience but is using a traditional male lens, and it operates by maintaining the status quo, you may wonder why there is a decline as new competitors open their eyes to the opportunity of using both lenses.

A male-dominated business where gender awareness is lacking is at the greatest risk of failing to see gender as a growth opportunity.

A traditional business may reject change because they are confused by some of the myths that surround it. They may not have experienced business hardship yet, but the speed with which women's economic power and influence are growing would indicate that a decline is imminent if they don't adjust their perspectives.

Businesses that choose to adopt the female lens will experience incremental growth. Typically, these businesses embrace women-omics; they have a perspective that allows them to see the changes that have occurred for women in the twentieth century. They are actively pursuing ways to connect to women through their products, communications, and internal and external cultures. They have the vision to see what is possible and the commitment to understanding how valuable women are in their business. They have powerful horizontal support and a deep vertical desire to really understand their consumers.

If you believe in a magic-bullet strategy, this is as close as you will get to it. In reality, as you will see, it is not going to be a 'quick fix' or overnight operation, but the rewards — yes, the profits — will make it more than worthwhile. So let's get down to it and look at how much money you could actually make...

CASE STUDY
AFL WOMEN'S LAUNCH

Jemma Wong, head of brand strategy and special projects @ AFL

OVERVIEW

In 2015, Australian Football League CEO Gillon McLachlan announced that the AFL would launch a national women's competition, fast-tracking plans from 2020 to 2017. This wasn't only a courageous moment for our game and the wider sports industry, it opened a new world of opportunity for the 350 000 girls and women who were playing the game at grassroots level. And even more, it signalled a new direction for the game — one that was more progressive, inclusive and ready to change. McLachlan announced, 'Equality and aspiration were big reasons for spending $4 million to set up the new competition. It was also good for business.'

In this league, women had always been a part of the game — on the supporter sidelines, inside the administration. At a community level, women were playing without the visibility and backing, professional input or media attention. While starting a professional female code wasn't about creating a 'female product for a female audience', we knew AFL Women's had the potential to mobilise our female supporters in an entirely new way, giving them a sense of ownership and opening up new revenue streams.

Compared to the established men's competition, the challenge of marketing this game was two-fold.

1. Brand challenge — How to fascinate a nation beyond novelty? And how to shift perceptions to position women as credible, active agents in the game.

2. **Audience challenge** — This wasn't just a 'build it and they will come' scenario. We had to convert our existing — somewhat sceptical — fan base as well as inspire a new audience.

THE OPPORTUNITY

This was more than marketing a professional league or competition. The women's product was an opportunity:

- to build a positive, female and inclusive culture across the entire industry

- to demystify female athletes and women in the game

- to create 200-plus empowered female heroes in sport

- to build new rituals and new types of belonging — for young boys, to look up to our female players and not only recognise but celebrate their talents; and for young girls, to never again disqualify themselves or take themselves out of the race.

COLLABORATION, NOT INSTRUCTION

Looking at the game through an authentic female lens, rather than from a traditional sports view, we didn't instruct, we *collaborated* to build a meaningful narrative around women in the AFL. We embarked on six months of education, inspiration and consultation with clubs, staff, players and partners, providing the context to the brand and audience strategy and having open discussions about the cultural change we could effect. A successful launch meant we needed our partners to be on the right side of the message, from the beginning.

EARLY SIGNS

- In five months, we built 100 000 fans on Facebook and 27 000 fans on Instagram driven by organic interest and storytelling by the Opening Round weekend.

- Our social media audiences were 67 per cent female, and the largest audience group was the 18–34 age bracket.

- The Opening Round weekend had an attendance of 50 000 people.

- The first game welcomed a capacity crowd of 24 000 fans to Ikon Park, with thousands of fans unable to get into the grounds.

- Merchandise sold out early in the season and memberships grew for clubs overnight.

- The majority of fans at the first game were women (this trend has continued throughout the competition). Women supporting women — it was a beautiful thing to see firsthand.

WHAT CAN OTHER BRANDS DO TO ATTRACT WOMEN?

- You need senior advocates who not only rationally understand the benefits but emotively connect. Emotion is where you'll see mindset shifts.

- Show the market opportunity with research, qualitative and quantitative data points.

- Have a tailored go-to-market strategy based on the right insight, the right channels, right time.

- Take the time to provide context for the female economy inside your organisation. This won't be solved in one presentation; it needs continual discussion and championing.

FEMALE FACTS

FACT: Neuroscience shows that women are a more engaged audience than men.

BENEFIT: *Increasing engagement with the biggest spender, leading to greater profits.*

FACT: Gender-specific marketing actually works much works harder because it ensures deeper and more insightful connections with an audience.

BENEFIT: *Establishing a deeper emotional relationship, leading to greater loyalty and commitment.*

FACT: Anyone at all, male or female, can learn how to deliver better and stronger business messages that women will love.

BENEFIT: *Becoming multi-lensed or bi-focally clever about gender, actually leads to better marketing focus and success.*

CHAPTER 7

$HOW ME THE MONEY

Business is about serving a purpose — providing employment, filling a need in the market and greasing the wheels of the economy. But mostly it is about making money.

Women account for 50 per cent of the population but they make 90 per cent of the decisions in many categories.[1] That's a lot of money to harness. So it's essential to establish how your business will attract these women into a fulfilling and long-term relationship with your brand.

Of course, it is also essential to expose what that relationship is worth to your business in an absolute dollar value. Money talks. Bottom line projections can get those not entirely convinced of the gender segmented discussion over the line and to start banking on the change to revenue opportunity. This chapter revolves around the actual value of the female economy that is available to you.

As we know, gender is a loaded topic that draws on all sorts of biases. One of the best things we can do is to get really objective and share potential revenue advantages and opportunities with our entire team to ensure everyone is on board with this process. Nothing motivates as much as more revenue and sales!

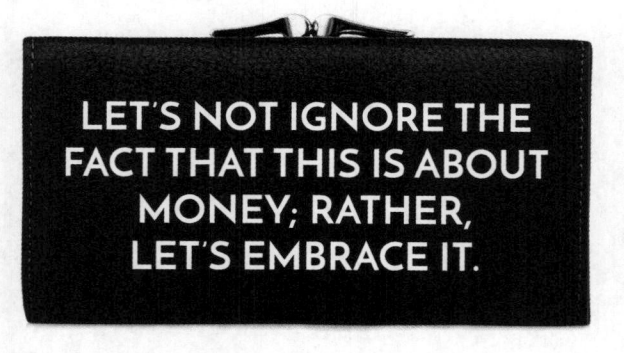

LET'S NOT IGNORE THE FACT THAT THIS IS ABOUT MONEY; RATHER, LET'S EMBRACE IT.

So, no more beating around the bush (we've been doing that as a society for far too long already). Let's start number crunching and finding out what is in your way right now when it comes to attracting the female audience.

4 STEP PROCESS

Finding out both the absolute dollar value and the market share available to your business, and identifying all the things standing between you and fully realising the female market, is as easy as the next 4 steps. It hinges on these questions:

1. What's the size of the prize?

2. What's in the way?

3. What's in your heart?

4. What lens are you using?

Let's walk through each step in detail.

STEP

1

2

3

4

1. WHAT'S THE SIZE OF THE PRIZE?

What is the dollar value of the female lens to your business?

How much can you potentially increase your revenue or sales, and decrease your attrition if you direct a dedicated focus on the female market?

The equation you need to apply is: **A – B = C**

A:	**FEMALE SALES AVAILABLE IN THE CATEGORY $XX (ACTUAL)**
	—
B:	**YOUR FEMALE SALES $YY (POTENTIAL)**
	=
C:	**THE SIZE OF THE PRIZE $ZZ**

Your final number is important because it will show you how viable a female-focused strategy is for your business. It will help inform what budget you should be prepared to invest to get the right traction. This will then lead you down the path covered in chapter 5 — from women flirting with your brand, to dating and purchasing more often, to tying the knot and making a commitment over the long term.

The next step is to analyse your data further:

1. Acquisition cost of female customers vs male customers. How much do you currently spend to win over a female customer and how does this differ to the cost of gaining a male customer? What would this tell us about current sales and marketing that we can use as leverage moving forward?

2. Retention rate of female vs male customers. Which gender is coming to your business the most? How long do they stay and why do they leave? How will you use this to inform your future strategy?

3. Average spend of female vs male customers. Who spends the most and the least? How can you use this information to make decisions to focus on the female market?

When you've seen all the data and examined it from every angle, you are ready to have a good look at your internal gender dynamics and how they affect your external gender dynamics.

2. WHAT'S IN THE WAY?

Is your business or organisation 'male behaviour dominant' or 'female behaviour dominant' in the way it operates both internally and externally? What are your KGIs (Key Gender Indicators)?

In chapter 3 we look at the different brain wiring and structure and the chemical hormonal differences of males and females. Now imagine you are looking at the brain of your business: are you operating like a male brain or like a female brain? Think of how a coach analyses an athlete's left-handed versus right-handed coordination. Most of us are more dominant on one side or the other. Like some superstars, you may be equally strong with left and right coordination, and this is a useful strength to uncover.

It's time to make some further assessments:

1. Organisational chart. What is the female/male ratio of your staff — from board and C-suite level all the way through the business to reception.

2. Financial costs of staff. What are the financial costs of your male staff versus your female staff? This includes overhead costs, salaries, bonuses and any other costs around male and female employees. This is not a witch-hunt for a gender wage gap, but it does tell us something about the overall culture of the business and where it stands on the evolutionary scale of gender awareness. This reality check is not for the faint-hearted, but for the very serious professionals who are determined to see profitable breakthroughs.

3. Human resources. What kind of gender awareness is already evident? Check in with your HR department, if you have one. Do you run gender-awareness programs, such as unconscious bias training, or diversity programs? Do you have hiring policies around gender? Are these working effectively? Is gender equity considered a 'women's issue' rather than a focus for all staff? Is any information missing on the gender culture that might be valuable to know? For example, is an overtly macho or alpha-male culture drowning out female voices? This is a good time to do a few qualitative interviews, and perhaps a quantitative study, depending on the size of your company.

Once you've examined your internal culture, you are ready to look externally to analyse the face you present to your customer and your community.

This audit is best undertaken by a skilled professional outside of your business who is free of influence or, dare we say, bias. This is exactly what I work through with clients, objectively assessing the touchpoints of people outside your world interfacing with your brand.

An external audit involves a gender analysis of:

- **all external communications** — looking for language, tone of voice, persona, visual semiotics and codes, user experience and the sales journey on your website, store fit-out, social media, customer service centre, printed collateral and visual material

- **the customer shopping experience** — analysing your call centre, store and online experience from a gender perspective

- **previous customer research data and results** — assessing what the past can tell us, and what patterns are being repeated, have shifted or stand out as pertinent to gender.

When I work through this step with clients, I tabulate their responses and create a scorecard that we work through together to uncover the blind spots.

1

2

STEP
3

4

3. WHAT'S IN YOUR HEART?

The previous two steps are very analytical and left-brain processes. Step 3, by contrast, is used to balance out the facts and has a very right-brain orientation.

I like to do a quick 'reaction' test, which is a bit like the patellar reflex test, where the doctor taps a certain point below your knee with a tiny hammer.

Ask yourself:

What does your heart say about whether you are a female-based or male-based business?

This helps create some immediate clarity and can assist you a little later when making a 'full body scan'. I have produced an online diagnostic tool called 'Cardiology' to help uncover what's in the heart of your business. Clients use it to sort out their feelings.

This exercise will assess the big picture of what *you* think is really important in the business and needs to be focused on most immediately in order to bring about transformational change. You will identify the three most pressing issues that should be focused on in the next 12 months. Will gender be one of them?

The really interesting part of this exercise is seeing the results from individuals in your business. If entire teams undertake the exercise it also sheds light on how much alignment exists among team members, at different levels within the business and across all departments.

It can be a fast way to see how functional the business is and if your staff are cohesive and focused in the same direction. Or it can be a great individual resource to help you get the clarity around which blind spots to work on first. Make sure you note who is identifying gender in their top three issues and what rating they are giving it.

Use the Cardiology diagnostic to work out what business issues are your immediate priorities: http://cardiology.becbrideson.com

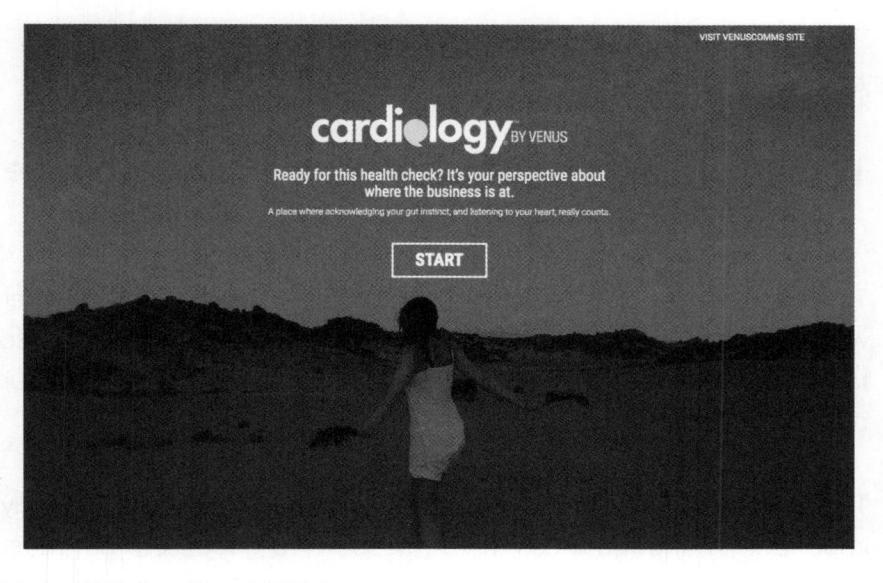

Use token number *9363* for access.

1

2

3

STEP
4

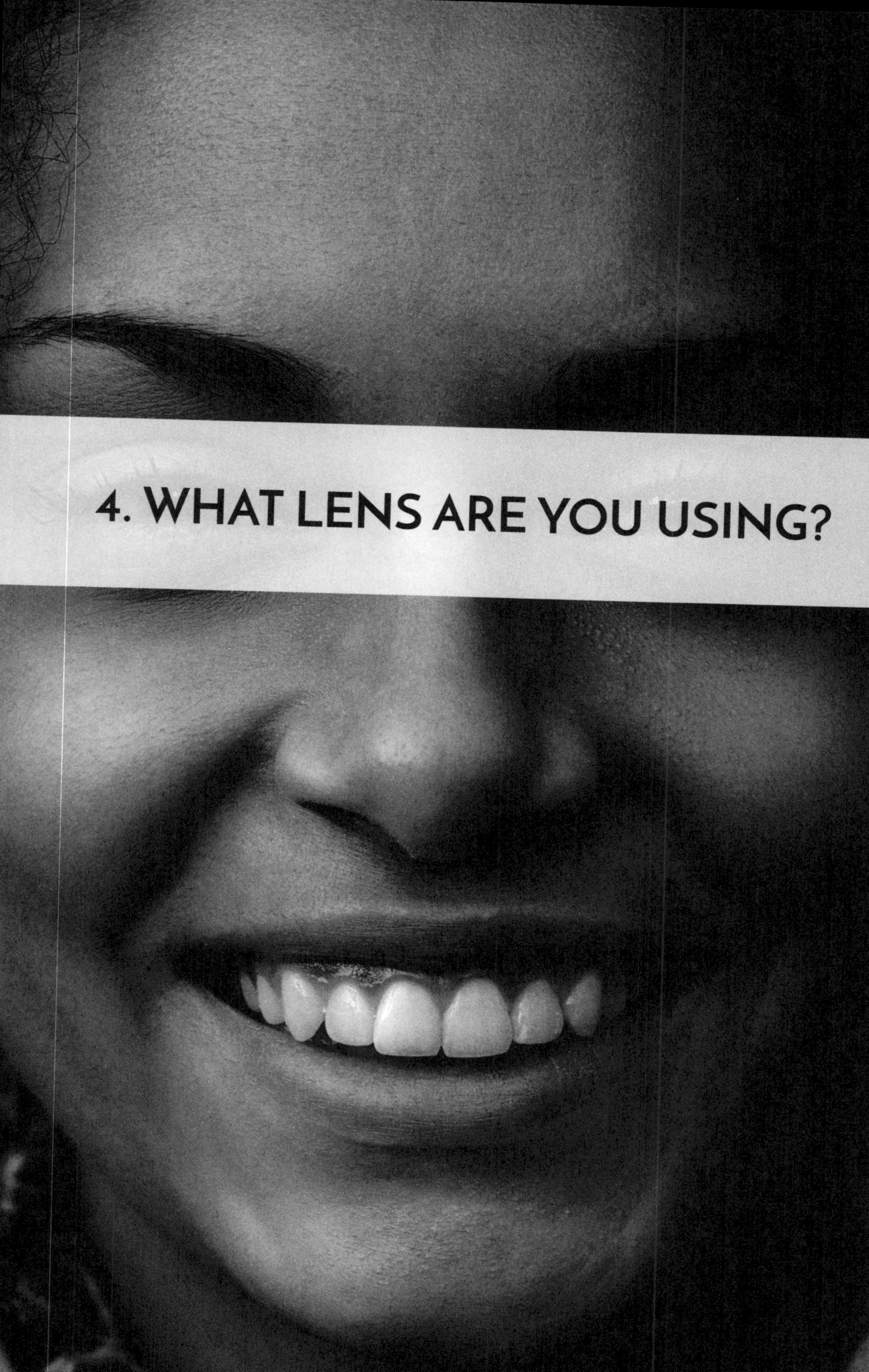

4. WHAT LENS ARE YOU USING?

In this step you draw conclusions from your results. Will you adopt a traditional lens or a female lens approach from this point on? In either case, this will need some robust discussion with your internal team.

Here are some questions you might ask:

- What did the numbers show and illuminate?

- What did the KGIs tell us? What did the internal and external gender preferences uncover about the business?

- What was surprising about these results?

- Thinking about all of the 'a-ha' moments throughout the process, how would you classify them?

- How aligned are your people and how will you develop the right working team to carry you forward?

Internal support and buy-in plays a big part in the success of your growth strategy. It is essential to have the right team in place, speaking a common language and with a common desire to understand the female commercial space.

When a CEO is involved, you know change is going to happen. If the leader of a business can see that point on the horizon, they will help create the pathway to ensure the business gets to the destination it is aiming for. If I am not working directly with the CEO, I always like to find out that he or she has 'skin in the game' and is committed to seeing the business through this process of 'gender-lensing'.

What leader would not want to see business growth and an increase in sales and revenue?

WHAT TO CHANGE, AND WHEN

There is no 'quick fix' to becoming more female focused. But there are some things you can look at changing in the short, medium and long term that will start to turn the ship around:

SHORT TERM – less effort, less impact

- collateral and some communications
- some minor product modifications/offers/deals
- persona and tone of voice

1

MID TERM – more effort, more impact

- communications in social media with strategic pillars
- sponsorship and media
- brand persona and personality
- sales floor staff and call centre training
- packaging updates
- strategic communications campaigns

2

LONG TERM – most effort, most impact

- new way of approaching research and insights, with a shift towards seeing it as a continuous effort to improve
- new approach to internal business operations/ departments and customer-centricity
- new fit-outs, stores, and head office appearance
- new communications and strategy rolled out across all business touchpoints
- inside out approach to female lens, creating authenticity.

3

KEEP MOVING

Changing your business so it becomes more gender-intelligent is a little like giving up smoking or going on a diet. You have to keep chipping away at it, and you never give up. It takes effort, but in time it becomes easier and more natural.

The day you make the pledge to do it, and start executing the micro-actions to see through the female lens, is the day your business begins its transformation.

There are times when gender bias blocks all progress and is the main obstacle to the business making more money. In the next chapter, we'll look at how you can overcome this obstacle.

CHAPTER 8

FUTURE PROOF AND FEMALE READY

Crack a safe and you can unlock the riches within. This is what you do when you begin to look at your business from the perspective of gender.

You're like a detective searching for clues. Often it's the smallest piece of evidence that can provide the biggest breakthrough.

A seemingly insignificant insight or piece of business intelligence could be the very thing that leads to you cracking that safe. Just because it's something 'small' does not mean it's not worth the investment. It's usually the stuff you have to search around for that changes your whole approach and delivers tenfold results.

It does not mean forgetting who you are as a business. This is not about starting a whole new way of working, but rather about adjusting your aperture to focus on your potential female customers, and to approach them in the right way.

You're taking evidence from your research, putting it through the lab tests and producing an amazing reimagined blueprint or wo-manifesto for your future growth.

There are three stages to adopting a 'female-lensed' transformation to boost your bottom line:

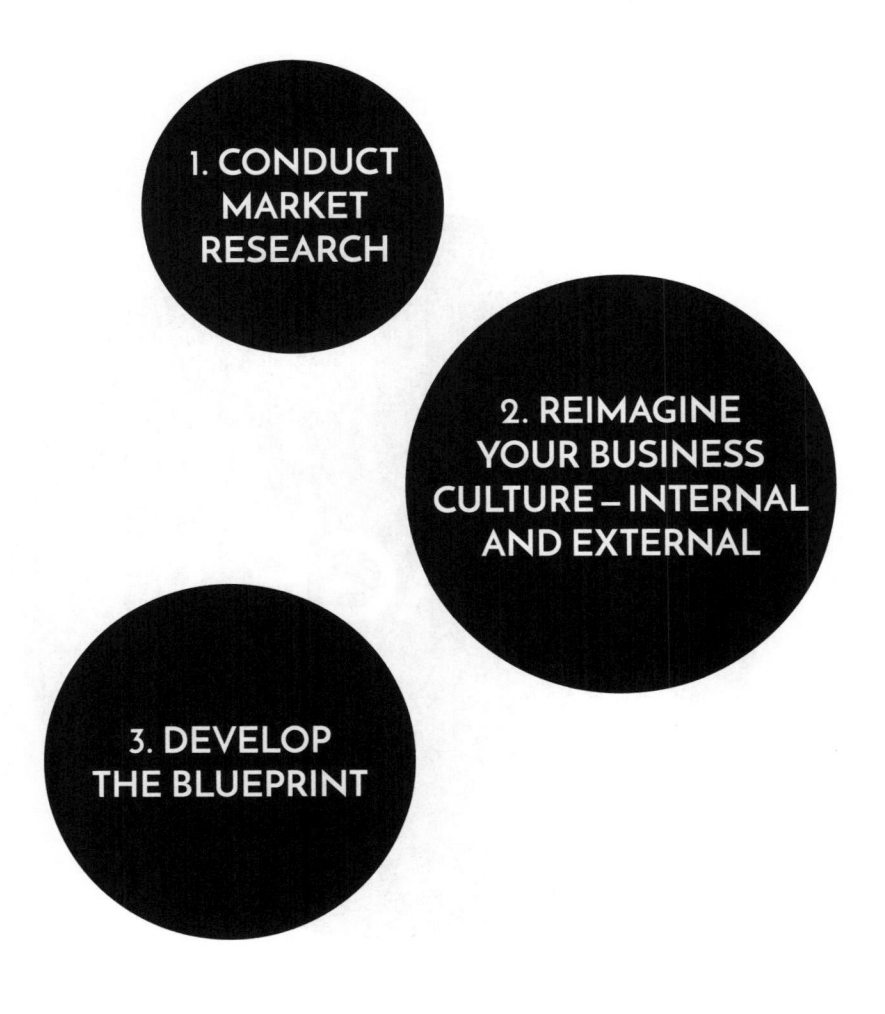

Let's look at each stage in order.

STAGE 1

CONDUCT MARKET RESEARCH

STAGE 1: CONDUCT MARKET RESEARCH.

When you're trying to understand your audience there is no better way of connecting with them than by actually talking to them. Too many businesses fail to do this! You need to ask them what they want and how they really feel about what you're offering.

Using pedestrian market research, or relying on a research methodology from the past, is a bit like seeing a general practitioner for a specialist problem. They might be able to identify the symptoms, but they are not trained to look for the underlying reasons they exist. Researchers who are not specialists in understanding women within your category or industry from a female perspective won't know how to diagnose your conditions, which will deny you the granular detail you need.

To continue to throw the same types of research questions at the same target market and expect different answers is a waste of resources.

One quality I have observed in researchers who unearth new insights is a willingness to forget what they think they know and to adopt an open mind. Drawing male-lensed conclusions on what is causing the symptoms is not the kind of deep listening that leads to intimate knowledge of women.

Creating a strategy to grow female markets requires deep listening and expert analysis. Over the years, I have seen lucid hypotheses shut down reflexively by teams who have been treading the same path too long. They are often blinkered to the possibilities of what could be, completely missing the scope and nuance of the bigger picture or a different approach.

One way to overcome this blindness is to work with academic consultants who can bring expert analysis and deep knowledge to the problem, just as Dove did when they adopted their 'start from day one' approach. In their quest for fresh insights beyond stale category clichés and responses, they dropped the old process and introduced a completely new methodology.

HUNCH VERSUS HYPOTHESIS

Dove had a hunch that the existing portrayals of beauty were thwarting women's desire to connect with one another, to foster positive self-esteem, and to relate to the communication and advertising images that were being delivered by an entire old-lensed industry.

To prove their hypothesis they developed a methodology that allowed them to discover what beauty really meant to modern women. The company collaborated with academics from Harvard University and the London School of Economics. The resulting study, aptly named 'The Real Truth about Beauty', explored women's feelings around beauty and wellbeing.[1] Specifically, they noted the relationship between women's outward appearance and their emotional and psychological health.

The study asked questions that hadn't been asked before. They addressed the real issues around women's perceptions about the communications that were being used to appeal to them. Which according to Dove's research was well off the mark, putting images out there that only reinforced female's inadequacies. They found that in the beauty category, for instance, that only 2 per cent of women thought they were beautiful.

Dove's hunch paid off. The work and the campaign have enjoyed more than a decade of brilliant results. Two further global research studies continued to deliver illuminating insights that informed Dove's approach to market.

Aside from positive trending sales results that have tracked to over $4 billion from $2.5 billion in its inaugural year,[2] Dove has also served a greater good for the community of women. Dove continues to use real women in advertising and marketing campaigns and to embrace a policy of 'no airbrushing'.[3] And the Dove Self-Esteem Project has positively affected the lives of more than 19 million young people across 128 countries through self-esteem education and training.[4]

MORE
HEART

LESS
HEAD

As consumers and customers, we do not think about brands rationally; fundamentally, we purchase and engage with a brand according to how we feel about it.

An unlikely breakthrough moment for me came when working on a frozen meal product that was well into the maturity phase of its life cycle and had been market researched over the years following the same old, well-worn and predictable path. Research over decades showed a pattern of repeated questions that produced similar insights that led to predictable minor incremental changes in sales and marketing. The product was losing traction and market share.

In an effort to understand the decline and what was turning consumers off, my team went into the retail environment with these women and analysed the emotions behind their rejection.

We found that they had an instinctive gut reaction to placing the product in their basket. They were filled with dread, shame, embarrassment and negative self-dialogue. Underneath these feelings they associated 'convenience' with laziness, culinary ineptitude or a perception of loneliness and social exclusion — a meal for one — and not even a self-made meal with fresh love in the ingredients, but a pre-made factory meal. No steamed green vegetables or 15-minute Jamie Oliver healthy meals, so the self-flagellation went on for these buyers. And this was the breakthrough moment in understanding where the category had a systemic problem that needed addressing. Without the analysis of this moment we might never have identified the hidden barrier to purchase. It was like discovering the smoking gun.

This is why you need more heart and less head when it comes to research.

Without the right ingredients, it's hard to get a recipe right. Research, and the insights you can gain from it, is a lot like that. Empathy based on a deep knowledge about women — that's what women really want.

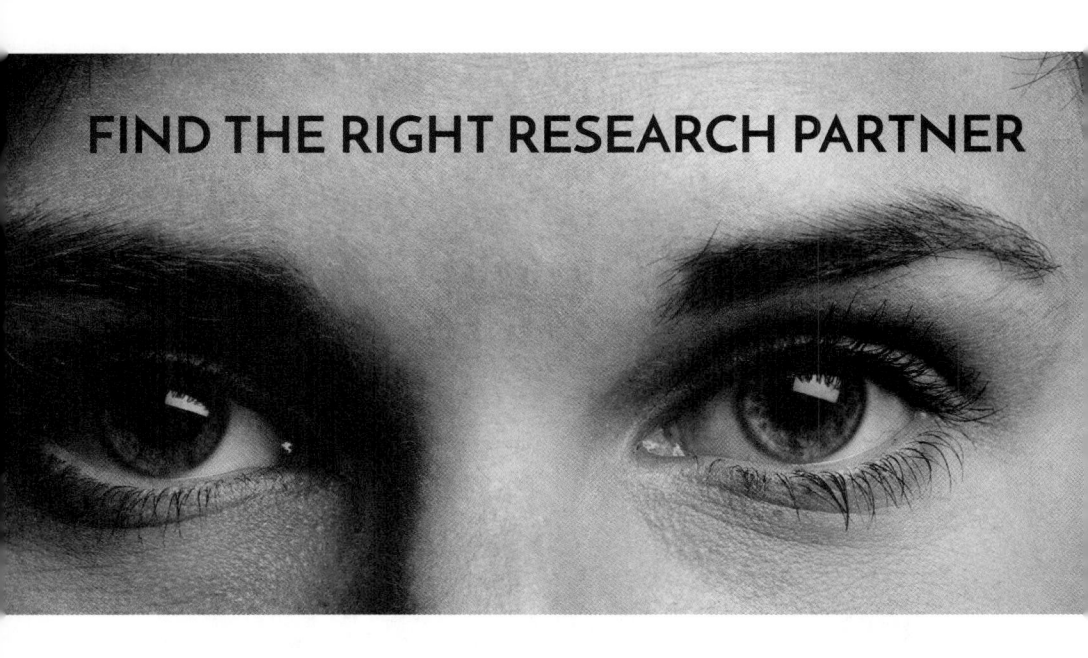

FIND THE RIGHT RESEARCH PARTNER

- Do they believe in and understand women and gender differences? Or are they traditionalists/generalists?

- Are they willing to partner with external experts in the category?

- What experience/affinity do they already have in this category? Is this a good or a bad thing? Are they relying too much on what they think they already know, rather than listening with fresh ears and looking with open eyes? Are they cutting corners because of this?

- Can they invest in this project over a decade and come on a long-game journey? Remember, this is about continuous and ongoing improvements. It is an iterative process.

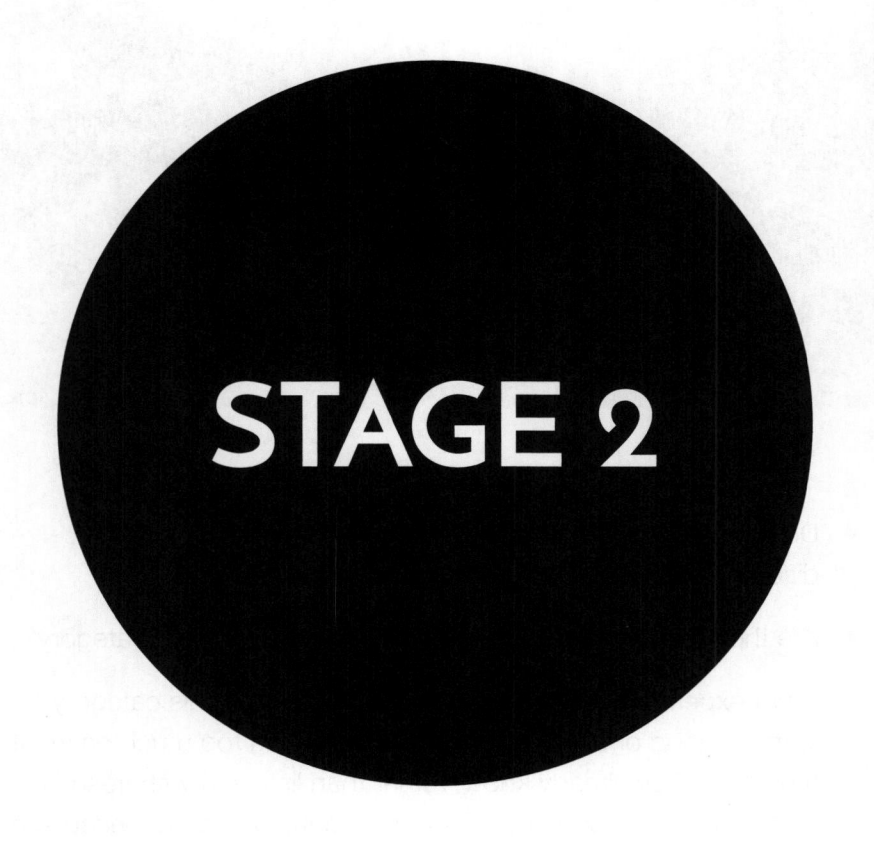

STAGE 2

REIMAGINE YOUR BUSINESS CULTURE – INTERNAL AND EXTERNAL

STAGE 2: REIMAGINE YOUR BUSINESS CULTURE – INTERNAL AND EXTERNAL

Constructing an environment that supports and understands the importance of females to the success of a business is about creating a set of values, an attitude and a code of behaviours. Together these factors foster a gender-intelligent culture.

Such a culture is created through a genuine commitment to study, understand and meet the needs of women. It is about legitimately setting about creating the change that recognises the role women play in the economy today.

Your business has an internal and an external culture. The external culture is more likely to be successful once the internal is effectively transformed.

1. REIMAGINE INTERNAL CULTURE

This book was not written through the eyes of a human resources professional. Rather, I'm a communications expert who started her own agency, ran her own female-focused business, and empowered lots of women and men by doing so.

I won't touch on all the functions of HR, but your HR department (if you have one) must be working with the rest of the business symbiotically in this area. It's about using your emotional intelligence and your business intelligence to create the right culture to attract women to your business, which is also known as gender-intelligence.

To help you make your fortune in the female economy, here is a six-point snapshot of the kind of culture that I have seen produces the best thinkers, the most empathetic people and the brightest talents.

i. Encourage career progression. Make this the norm. Act with transparency and help create visible pathways for performance. Importantly, keep the dialogue open about where she's at and what she needs, so you can partner with her in meeting her own milestones of progress.

ii. Hire talent, provide experience. Some people have not had the same advantages as others. Don't let that stand in the way, because talent, intelligence and ambition top privilege, networks and nepotism every time.

iii. Make business a second home. We spend much of our time in the office, so are the creature comforts in place? Is there a family-friendly breastfeeding room, a time-out space, kitchen amenities and clean bathrooms? Little things are a big deal.

iv. Be human. We all have bad days, strained personal relationships, emotional wounds and our own stories. These don't need to come to work with us every day but we need to know that the human stuff is okay.

v. Educate everyone about diversity. This is not 'a woman's problem', it's a business opportunity. Actively pursue gender smart training, especially for those who say 'we don't have that problem here.'

Don't make feelings something women bring to work but then have to hide in the bottom drawer with their handbag.

vi. See it, be it. She's not 'one of the boys' and it's a trap for women to adapt their behaviour so they can join the club. It's okay to be different. It's great to have strong cultures that support each other, with men and women considered equally. How do you foster an environment where she can survive without having to subjugate her values, and where her non-attendance when the men get messy at the local pub after work doesn't mean she is excluded from the business?

...GINE EXTERNAL CULTURE

...create an external female-lensed culture on three levels
...1):

...es.

...art.

...us.

...creating a female-lensed external culture

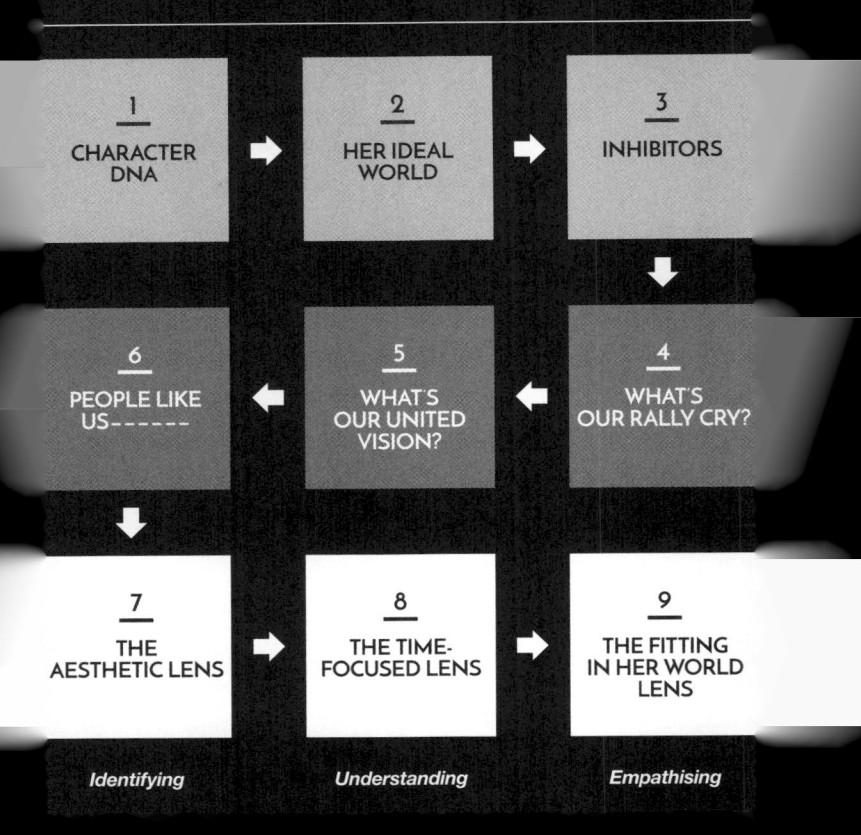

1 CHARACTER DNA →	**2** HER IDEAL WORLD →	**3** INHIBITORS ↓
6 PEOPLE LIKE US‐‐‐‐‐‐ ←	**5** WHAT'S OUR UNITED VISION? ←	**4** WHAT'S OUR RALLY CRY?
↓ **7** THE AESTHETIC LENS →	**8** THE TIME-FOCUSED LENS →	**9** THE FITTING IN HER WORLD LENS
Identifying	*Understanding*	*Empathising*

IN HER
SHOES

As the adage goes, to 'walk a mile in her shoes' is to understand and empathise with her personal lived experience.

You need to profile her character and her life — where she lives, works, studies and plays, and the many variables in her life. Much like any new relationship, you're building up a portrait of her character to get to know her and build empathy.

Imagine what she is doing, thinking and feeling about life, about the world and, importantly, about where your business fits into all of this. What does she expect from where you intersect in her life?

For example, imagine you are a healthy frozen food company and she relies on your products to feed her family during really busy times in her life. She expects healthy food, value for money and convenience around the purchase. The freezers are cold, so make the packaging easy to navigate. She's obviously time poor, so make microwaving simple. But don't treat her like a fool who can't cook. She's cutting corners for a reason — respect that.

Equally important is to assess what's hampering your relationship. What is happening in your business and industry that really gets in the way of her being able to realise her ideal world?

In the case of frozen food, if the food doesn't deliver, the packaging turns her off, the brand doesn't speak to her or recognise her unique situation, and she feels invisible, then you can expect a 'tolerated' relationship to be short-lived.

IN HER
HEART

You have to understand her feelings and show her that you are aware of her goals and ambitions. And also explore what's behind her rational decision to spend time with your business.

In sales, this is about creating affinity with your customer and getting on 'the same side of the table' as her. What is it about your business and brand that she needs and wants, and how do you team up with her to deliver it? What do you both believe in? How would you articulate and use that shared belief?

This is really important for creating affinity in areas that will bind your business to her in a wedlock of understanding.

Eating frozen meals should not make her feel that she's lazy, hopeless or lonely. Her choice to buy into the frozen-food category simply means she needs a product that helps her prioritise other things in her busy lifestyle such as career, hobbies and social events while maintaining a healthy diet. Bring her this positive insight and you'll have smashed the stereotype.

IN HER
FOCUS

Make sure you are visible in her physical world in a way that resonates with her so she wants to relate to you.

To attract women, one of the most important aspects of your business marketing is the aesthetics of your brand. Women's brains are finely attuned to their physical environment. The image of your brand is the first place she will make a quick gut judgement on both what your business is about and whether you're worth entering into a relationship with.

Beyond superficial appearances, the aesthetics and semiotics of a brand help women to decode the values of your business. Aesthetics in product categories can become monotonous and formulaic. In creating a female-lensed business culture, the importance of this part of the process cannot be underestimated.

Having the right design team is as important as having the right research team. Understanding how to curate the brand and to consistently present it authentically is the key to unlocking the brand's greatest potential in the female market.

As we see in chapter 4, time is a massive factor for modern women. How can your business provide her with more quality time? Every time she interfaces with your brand you need to add value to the experience or find a way to expedite the process so you give her back time for things that matter to her. So how will your business take these insights and help your time-poor female customers?

The final piece of the female-lensed business culture is to understand where you fit in her life. When is she likely to think about, discover and interact with your business category? What are the touchpoints? How will she feel about you when you are in her field of vision? This may include considering where you are physically and what mediums you use to communicate through.

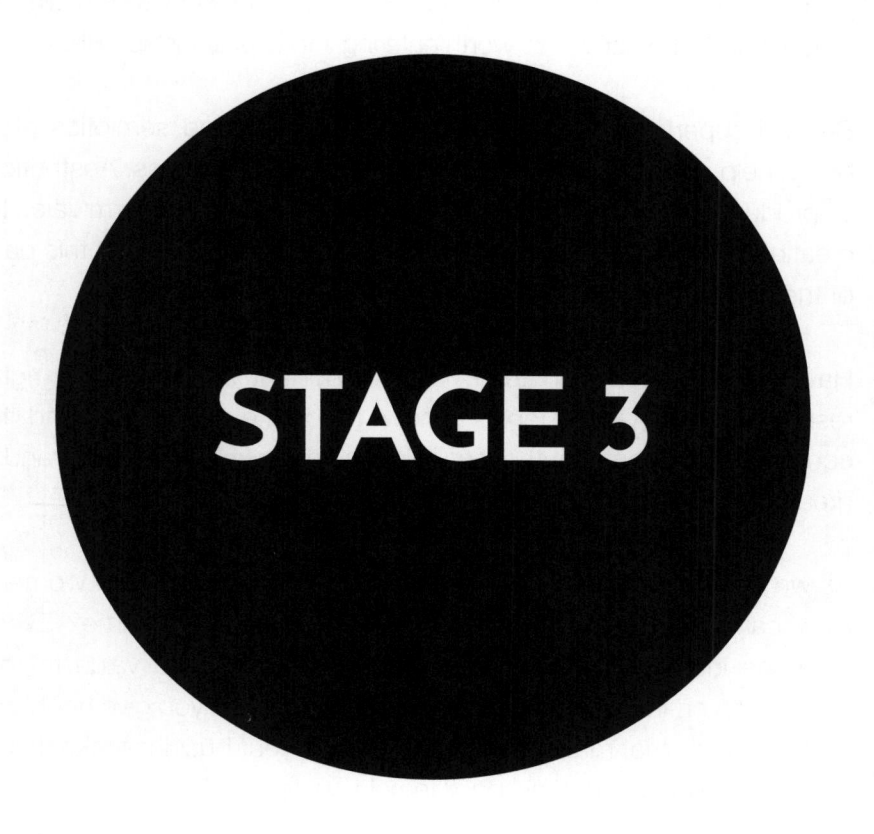

STAGE 3

DEVELOP
THE BLUEPRINT

STAGE 3: DEVELOP THE BLUEPRINT

When renovating a house, an architect consults with the owners, listens to their needs, and notes their ideas and insights, before planning and submitting rough designs for approval. After this follows a rigorous process of working out exactly how the design elements can be brought together in the new home. This is your blueprint.

Creating a female-lensed business is a little like renovating an existing structure by bringing in new design features. Many parts of the existing building will be retained and even enhanced. Shore up the foundations, rewire and replaster, add a new roof and kitchen. All this takes time and happens in phases.

Figure 8.2 shows the three phases of implementing a strong, gender-intelligent blueprint:

1. growth   2. advantage   3. innovation and leadership.

Figure 8.2: three phases to business leadership

Growth (12–18 months)

- new product design and development launched to market successfully
- overhaul of brand semiotics and communication (style and techniques) with the market
- cultural shift within the business and an engaged and energised workforce around the newfound channel of growth
- clear and concise communication with all internal and external suppliers to embrace the blueprint and become valued partners in the journey.

Advantage (18 months–3 years)

- a spike in sales, customer acquisition, and retention of new and existing customers
- more emotional and intellectual advantage over your competition, because you have provided a brand culture that she is 'married to' and you understand the market conditions in ways your competitors can only dream of
- positive brand recognition and sentiment
- engaged, committed workforce focused on ongoing leverage of the market position you have gained
- competitors in the market either losing ground or playing 'copy-cat' to try to survive the market pressure your business has produced.

Innovation and leadership (3 years +)

- established leader in category with first mover advantage
- stable customer loyalty, which means you can venture into new territory, create brand extensions or spinoffs with the credibility you have earned
- scale and size is now on your side, allowing you to continue market domination.

You must communicate your blueprint throughout the business so all those involved with the renovation can share the vision of the end result. This process is critically important to ensuring that the business plan is accepted, understood and embraced.

Distilling, designing and disseminating the vision is the way we share the renaissance that the business will undergo. It provides the proof and triggers the shift that will become more than words or values on T-shirts and coffee mugs.

Your blueprint becomes the vehicle to spread the adapted culture and creates meaning for your people. It gives them an understanding of the essence of your female lens and injects life into the vision at all levels.

Have you noticed how important storytelling has become as a business tool? Being able to articulate your female-lensed vision in a way that is relevant and insightful to the business and its history is key. When communicated internally, it must be easy to understand and relate to. It must not alienate the internal team or create gender segregation, but rather create a place that brings genders together for the greater good of the business and its financial success.

Getting all three parts of this vision right will be the beginning of a long relationship with loyal, cashed-up and in-love female consumers.

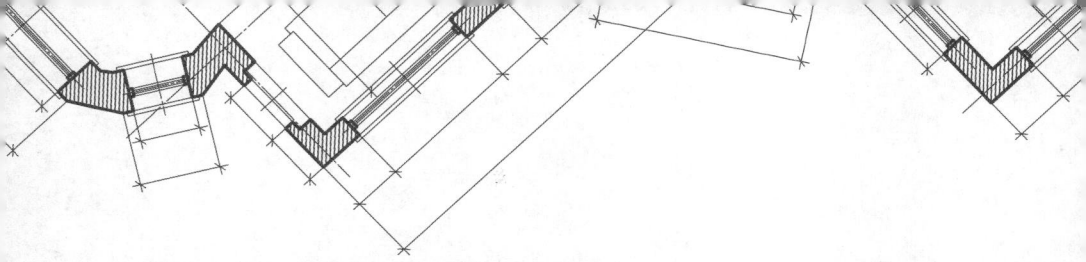

TRANSITION AND TRANSFORM

Long-term, lasting engagement of female consumers means more than a fancy coffee-table book in your reception with incredible tales of inspiring women and motivational words from those long-passed. It's a commitment to a relationship with women and a tangible action plan moving forward.

The behaviourist psychologist Jean Piaget explains adaptation in terms of *assimilation* and *accommodation*.[5] For example, a child may see a zebra and call it a horse; because it looks like the horses she has seen, she assimilates it into her schema for a horse. But when she is told the stripes make it a different animal called a zebra, she adapts her understanding in light of this new information — that is accommodation.

Transforming your business involves getting the accommodation right. To do this successfully, your blueprint must be spot-on. You must have buy-in from everyone in your organisation, including your human resources and management teams.

You must be committed and understand you are playing a long game, not looking for short-term gains.

Only then will you address all of the blind spots, become a truly forward-thinking organisation and begin to future proof your biggest asset.

CONCLUSION

Imagine the things we take for granted because that's just the way they are: things like the weather, water ... and news.

It was only in the 1940s in the US that TV news went from being broadcast twice a week to featuring every night.[1] Back then, with television station licences still limited, it was a very different medium from what we know today, but generally the news still follows the same sequential format it always has: breaking news of the day, current events and political news, sports news and the weather.

The genesis of this was the newspaper, of course. The headlines that interested the men who would be buying and reading it — news on one side, sport on the other. Women had their magazines with recipes, knitting patterns and society gossip.

Over time the television news desk changed, the set design revisited every few years, graphics and digital broadcasting becoming ever more sophisticated. Yet the format is still roughly two-thirds news and one-third sport and weather.

It made sense in the 1960s, when most women worked unpaid in the home and were usually busy cooking dinner at news time. Hubby came home to his pipe and slippers, read the newspaper and watched the television (as more homes could afford them). The 30-minute program that aired, while she prepared the evening meal, consisted of information from a male perspective on news that men typically showed an interest in.

If networks were to investigate how they might engage more female viewers, then they might consider a different format. Through a female lens, it might instead look like early general news, current affairs, weather and an update on the latest in education, emotional intelligence, or even enlightenment on social issues.

Given the decline in traditional television viewing audiences the networks are facing, perhaps a new approach at this point in history would prove fruitful?

Here's a wonderful example of what the female lens can achieve. A group of Australian women, married to vegetable farmers, convened regularly to discuss the business side of their husbands' farms, bringing to it their wide range of professional experience in the disciplines of law, accounting, marketing and education. Yet they had been applying the same traditional lens to issues around the administration and governance of their husbands' businesses.[2]

Then an interesting thing happened. After a trip to the United States in search of a solution to the problem of 10 per cent stock wastage, they switched lenses and approached the problem from the viewpoint of wives and mothers.

The farmers grew carrots and sold them to the big retailers for $1000 a tonne, but quality standards meant any that were misshapen or irregular were diverted to stock feed, sold at just $50 a tonne. Once these women had set their plan in motion, the carrots previously sold as 'waste' were repurposed as a new $500 a tonne product. That's a 900 per cent increase in value.

Lunchboxes and food preparation are common concerns in the modern woman's life. The demand to fill fussy little tummies day after day was an ongoing concern for mothers. Now, thanks to these clever women, they had the opportunity to buy fresh carrots, already peeled, washed, chopped into a variety of shapes and packaged. Just open the bag and use! For preparation time and convenience, we'd call that a smart solution and a viable business opportunity, thanks to the lens change.

THIS IS WHAT YOU NOW NEED TO DO

Here you are, at the end of the book, poised to deliver to a ready market of women what they want in their ideal world. Future growth looks assured. Now you must make sure that this precious idea successfully passes all the milestones along the road to realisation.

Your gender-intelligent business culture will need to be visible and visceral and felt and experienced at all the touchpoints of your business. It is all these moments of truth that will connect women to your brand with deep authenticity and understanding.

Remember, you need to get the audience of women who may have ignored or at best tolerated you to spend time with your business, to feel the difference and to decide to make a commitment to you.

Imagine the team of people you will need to realise your own version of this 'rescue renovation'. They will need to be the best, because there will be a strong correlation between the team that helps you get there and what you finally deliver to your female audience.

Probably you will find it is a lot more complex than you first thought, but I believe in you. I believe you can open your eyes and focus on addressing each and every one of your blind spots.

Good luck.

7 $ECRET$ TO FEMALE$

1. Alignment

You share a common vision and values. You have seen into her life and acted in a way that helps rather than hinders her.

2. Product fit

Do you need to produce a new product or innovate and reimagine the one you have? Don't 'pink and shrink it', but provide the meaningful benefits she is looking for and a differentiation your competitors are blind to.

3. Price and value

Women can be sold on price, but only once they like you. Create a business that means more than the price tag. Love is blind to dollar signs, so make sure she loves you.

4. Community

Develop a way to fit in her community, connect her with like-minded women and become 'one of the girls'. Even brands can be besties.

5. Location

You're 'always on' because women live a 24-hour life online. Make your 'window' look appealing, keep her coming back to your online presence and don't forget she can now curate her own news feed on social media.

6. Diversity

That means all shapes, sizes, genders, races and abilities. When the community is aligned, everyone is winning.

7. Understanding

Avoid clumsy sales or marketing 'spray and pray'. It must feel authentic right through the business, based on deep insights, not a token effort to pay lip-service to women.

It's a big, bold and audacious vision, isn't it?

To suggest that maybe there is a new way in which to approach your business and brand.

To actually pull apart what we have learned about gender, to re-examine then rebuild the kinds of relationships that people really seek.

So now the blind spots have been illuminated, where will you begin?

At the start, of course! Revisit the parts of this book that really spoke to you. Write in the margins, underline and fill it with thoughts on practical tools and strategies. Work out some figures — the real financial reason you must start operating through this new perspective. Look at the dollars you are potentially missing out on.

If you want more inspiration or help, get in touch and we'll work together to address your specific needs. That could begin with a speaking engagement, a workshop or a secondment to your organisation. There's no surer path to transformation than to implement changes in person.

I hope this is just the start of a long relationship between us, and in practising what I preach, I welcome your feedback, ideas and thoughts.

Bec
@becbrideson
becbrideson.com

Send

REFERENCES

INTRODUCTION

1. Major, N. (2013). *Women: The Next Emerging Market*. [online] London: Ernst & Young Women. Available at: ey.com (accessed 10 April 2017).
2. Pofeldt, E. (2015). 'Women's Entrepreneurship and Innovation Surge Globally'. [online] *Forbes*. Available at: forbes.com (accessed 10 April 2017).
3. Silverstein, M. & Sayre, K. (2009). 'The Female Economy'. [online] *Harvard Business Review*. Available at: hbr.org (accessed 10 April 2017).
4. Roth, M. (2016). 'Women Make Up 85% of All Consumer Purchases'. [online] Bloomberg. Available at: bloomberg.com (accessed 10 April 2017).
5. Cavanaugh, B. (2007). 'Women's Work: MassMutual's directive to bring more women into financial services is changing how women look at the industry, and vice versa'. *Best's Review*. Available at: ambest.com (accessed 10 April 2017).
6. Pofeldt, op. cit.
7. Major, op. cit.
8. Price, S & Williams, J. (2017). *PWC Women in Work Index*. [online] London; PWC. Available at: pwc.co.uk (accessed 10 April 2017).

CHAPTER 1

1. Yankelovich (2014). *Yankelovich Monitor*. Norwalk, Connecticut: Yankelovich.
2. Alvarado, U. (2014). 'The Origin of the Marketing Concept'. [online] *Uriel*. Available at: uriel.org (accessed 10 April 2017).
3. Brian Jones, D. & Shaw, E. (2003). 'The History of Marketing Thought'. In: R. Weitz & R. Wensley, eds, *Handbook of Marketing*. 1st ed. London: SAGE Publications, p. 50.

4. Lamb, V. (2011). *The 1950s and the 1960s and the American Woman: The transition from housewife to feminist.* [online] HAL. Available at: dumas.ccsd.cnrs.fr (accessed at 10 April 2017).

5. Roper, M. (1994). *Masculinity and the British Organisation Man since 1945.* London: Oxford University Press, pp. 116 –17.

6. Foley, T. (2012). 'Women and Work'. [online] History Link. Available at: historylink.org (accessed 10 April 2017).

7. Hartog, H. (2002). *Man and Wife in America: A History.* Boston: Harvard University Press, pp. 189–90.

8. Rosin, H. (2010). 'The End of Men'. [online] *The Atlantic.* Available at: theatlantic.com (accessed 10 April 2017).

9. Foley, op. cit.

10. FABS (2011). *Births, Australia, 2010: Median Average for Parents.* [online] Australia: ABS. Available at: abs.gov.au (accessed 10 April 2017).

11. ABS (2015). *Births registered, Summary Statistics for Australia.* [online] Australia: ABS. Available at: abs.gov.au (accessed 10 April 2017).

12. ABS (2015). *A Profile of Australian Women in Business.* [online] Australia: ABS for the Office for Women. Available at: dpmc.gov.au (accessed 10 April 2017).

13. Silverstein, M., Sayre, K. & Butman, J. (2009). *Women Want More: How to Capture Your Share of the World's Largest, Fastest-Growing Market.* US: Harper Business.

14. See Yankelovich, op. cit.; Arnolds (2002). *Arnold's Women Insight Team.* Boston: Greenfield Online; Association of National Advertisers (2017). *Reality Check: New Equality Measure Targets Gender Bias in Ads and Media.* [online] Available at: businesswire.com (accessed 10 April 2017); Rosenberg G. (2014). 'Study: 91% of Women Feel Misunderstood by Advertisers'. [online] *Contentedly.* Available at: contentedly.com (accessed 10 April 2017).

15. Popcorn, F. & Marigold, L. (1996). *Clicking: 16 Trends to Future Fit Your Life, Your Work and Your Business*. US: Harper Business.
16. Popcorn, F. & Marigold, L. (2000). *Eveolution: Understanding Women — Eight Essential Truths That Work in Your Business and Your Life*. US: Harper Business.
17. Silverstein, M. & Sayre, K. (2009). 'The Female Economy'. [online] *Harvard Business Review*. Available at: hbr.org (accessed 10 April 2017).
18. Silverstein & Sayre, op. cit.
19. Silverstein, Sayre & Butman, op. cit.
20. See Martin, S. (2015). 'Gender Gap widens as women graduates outpace the men'. *The Australian.* [online] Available at: theaustralian. com.au (accessed 10 April 2017); Weale, S. (2016). 'UK's university gender gap is a national scandal, says thinktank'. *The Guardian*. [online] Available at: theguardian.com (accessed 10 April 2017); UN (2015). *The World's Women 2015: Trends and Statistics*. [online] New York: UN. Available: unstats.un.org (accessed 10 April 2017); Hepi (2016). *Boys to Men: The underachievement of younger men in higher education — and how to start tackling it*. [online] UK: Hepi. Available at: hepi.ac.uk (accessed 10 April 2017).
21. Rosin, op. cit.
22. Silverstein & Sayre, op. cit.
23. Arnolds, op. cit.
24. Gladwell, M. (2007). *Blink: The Power of Thinking Without Thinking*. US: Black Bay Books.
25. Silverstein & Sayre, op. cit.
26. Silverstein & Sayre, op. cit.
27. Hunt, V., Layton, D. & Prince, S. (2015). *Why Diversity Matters*. [online] McKinsey & Company. Available at: mckinsey.com (accessed 10 April 2017).

CHAPTER 2

1. Morrison, M. (2016). 'Gustavo Martinez Out at JWT; Tamara Ingram Tapped as Successor'. [online] *Advertising Age*. Available at: adage.com (accessed 10 April 2017).
2. Zarya, V. (2016). 'The Ex-CEO of J. Walter Thompson Makes a Rape Joke in a Newly Released Video'. [online] *Fortune*. Available at: fortune.com (accessed 10 April 2017).
3. Madansky, M. (2016). 'Elephant on Madison Avenue'. [online] The 3% Movement. Available at: elephantonmadisonavenue.com (accessed 10 April 2017).
4. O'Reilly, L. (2015). 'The 17 Richest People in Advertising, ranked by income'. [online] *Business Insider Australia*. Available at: businessinsider.com.au (accessed 10 April 2017).
5. O'Reilly, L. (2016). 'Saatchi & Saatchi chairman Kevin Roberts thinks the gender diversity in advertising debate is over'. [online] *Business Insider Australia*. Available at: businessinsider.com.au (accessed 10 April 2017).
6. O'Reilly, L. (2016). 'Saatchi and Saatchi chairman Kevin Roberts has resigned following his controversial gender diversity comments'. [online] *Business Insider Australia*. Available at: businessinsider.com.au (accessed 10 April 2017).
7. The 3% Conference (2013). *Female CDs on the Rise*. [online] New York City: The 3% Conference. Available at: 3percentconf. com (accessed 10 April 2017).
8. Dan, A. (2016). 'Why Aren't Women Starting Their Own Ad Agencies?' [online] *Forbes*. Available at: forbes.com (accessed 10 April 2017).
9. ABC News (2016). 'Australian Women Earn 23 per cent Less than Men, according to Workplace Equality Scorecard'. [online] *ABC News*. Available at: abc.net.au (accessed 10 April 2017).

10. Lyons, L. (2016). *Gender Equity Insights: Insider Australia's Gender Pay Gap* [online] WGEA. Available at: wgea.gov.au (accessed 10 April 2017).

11. Wadhwa, T. & Farquhar, P. (2016). 'Australia has continued its slide in the World Economic Forum's Annual Gender Gap Report'. [online] *Business Insider Australia*. Available at: businessinsider.com.au (accessed 10 April 2017).

12. Sanghani, R. (2016). 'Donald Trump is right — we're in denial about 'locker-room' banter'. [online] *The Telegraph*. Available at: telegraph.co.uk (accessed 10 April 2017).

13. *The Guardian* (2016). 'The full transcript of Michele Obama's powerful New Hampshire speech'. [online] *The Guardian*. Available at: theguardian.com (accessed 10 April 2017).

14. Mathis-Lilley, B. (2016). 'Trump was recorded in 2005 bragging about grabbing women "by the pussy"'. [online] *Slate*. Available at: slate.com (accessed 10 April 2017).

15. Al-Heeti, A (2017). 'Michelle Obama reminds tech industry — again-girls can code'. [online] CNET. Available at: cnet.com [Accessed 15 June. 2017]

16. McGregor, A. (2014). *Why Medicine Often Has Dangerous Side Effects For Women*. [video] TED. Available at: ted.com (accessed 10 April 2017).

17. McGregor, op. cit.

18. Peiss, K. (2011). *Hope in a Jar: The Making of America's Beauty Culture*. US: University of Pennsylvania Press.

19. Peiss, K. (1998). '"Vital Industry" and Women's Ventures: Conceptualising Gender in Twentieth Century Business History'. *Gender and Business,* 72 (2), pp. 219–41.

20. Silverstein, M. & Sayre, K. (2009). 'The Female Economy'. [online] *Harvard Business Review*. Available at: hbr.org (accessed 10 April 2017).

21. Hunt, H., Layton, D. & Prince, S. (2015). *Why Diversity Matters*. [online] Boston: McKinsey & Company. Available at: mckinsey.com (accessed 10 April 2017).

22. Noland, M., Moran, T. & Kotschwar, B. (2016). 'Is Gender Diversity Profitable? Evidence from a Global Survey'. [online] *Working Paper* 16 (3). Available at: piie.com (accessed 10 April 2017).

23. Carter, N., Joy, L., Wagner, H. & Narayanan, S. (2007). *The Bottom Line: Corporate Performance and Women's Representation on Boards*. [online] *Catalyst*. Available at: catalyst.org (accessed 10 April 2017).

24. Perry, G. (2014). 'The Rise and Fall of Default Man'. [online] *The New Statesman*. Available at: newstatesman.com (accessed 10 April 2017).

25. Price, R. (2016). '"Pokemon Go" is already bigger than Tinder, and it's about to overtake Twitter'. [online] *Business Insider Australia*. Available at: businessinsider.com.au (accessed 10 April 2017).

26. Friedman, U. (2015). 'How an Ad Campaign Invented the Diamond Engagement Ring'. [online] *The Atlantic*. Available at: theatlantic.com (accessed 10 April 2017).

27. Yee, B. (2003). 'Ads Remind Women They Have Two Hands'. [online] *The Wall Street Journal*. Available at: wsj.com (accessed 10 April 2017).

CHAPTER 3

1. Rose, T. (2013). *The Myth of Average*. [video] TED-Ed. Available at: ed.ted.com (accessed 10 April 2017).

2. Brizendine, L. (2006). *The Female Brain*. New York: Morgan Road Books.

3. Connor, S. (2013). 'The Hardwired Differences Between Male and Female Brains Could Explain Why Men Are Better at Map Reading'. [online] *Independent*. Available at: independent.co.uk (accessed 10 April 2017).

4. Khazan, O. (2013). 'Male and Female Brains Really Are Built Differently'. [online] *The Atlantic*. Available at: theatlantic.com (accessed 10 April 2017).

5. See Cunningham, J. (2012). *Inside Her Pretty Little Head: A New Theory of Female Motivation and What It Means for Marketing.* Australia: Marshall Cavendish International Pte; Barletta, M. (2007). *Marketing to Women.* US: Kaplan Publishing; Sax, L. (2006). *Why Gender Matters: What Parents and Teachers Need to Know about the Emerging Science of Sex Differences.* New York: Doubleday; Brizendine, op. cit.

6. Underhill, P. (1999). *Why We Buy: The Science of Shopping.* New York: Simon & Schuster.

7. Underhill, P. (2011). *What Women Want: The Science of Female Shopping.* New York: Simon & Schuster.

8. White, S. (2014). 'Meet the boss: Diana Williams'. *The Sydney Morning Herald.* [online] Available at: smh.com.au (accessed 10 April 2017).

9. McEncroe, G. (2017). *Shebah.* [online] Available at: shebah.com.au (accessed 10 April 2017).

10. Richardson, L. (2015). 'Bringing back the barber: 2015 hottest shaving trends'. *Australian Financial Review.* [online] Available at: afr.com (accessed 10 April 2017).

11. Sweeney, M. (2016). 'Unilever vows to drop sexist stereotypes from its ads'. [online] *The Guardian*. Available at: theguardian.com (accessed 10 April 2017).

12. Cramphorn, S. (2007). *Men are from Mars…when it comes to advertising*. [online] Melbourne: AddImpact. Available at: addimpact.net (accessed 10 April 2007).

13. Wedel, M. & Kamakura, W. (2000). *Market Segmentation*. US: Kluwer Academic Publishers, pp. 3–6.

14. Park, G. (2016). 'Women are warmer but no less assertive than men: Gender and Language on Facebook'. [online] *PLoS One*, 11(5). Available at: journals.plos.org (accessed 10 April 2017).

CHAPTER 4

1. Bahadur, N. (2014). 'Dove "Real Beauty" Turns 10: How a Brand Tried To Change the Conversation about Real Beauty'. [online] *Huffington Post*. Available at: huffingtonpost.com.au (accessed 10 April 2017).
2. Silverstein, M., Sayre, K. & Butman, J. (2009). *Women Want More: How to Capture Your Share of the World's Largest, Fastest-Growing Market*. US: Harper Business.
3. UN (2015). 'Facts and Figures: Economic Empowerment'. [online] UN Women. Available at: unwomen.org (accessed 10 April 2017).
4. *Daily Mail* (2014). 'Mothers get just 17 minutes a day to themselves'. [online] *Daily Mail*. Available at: pressreader.com (accessed 10 April 2017).
5. Popcorn & Marigold, op. cit.

CHAPTER 5

1. Warner, F. (2002). 'Nike Women's Movement'. [online] *Fast Company*. Available at: fastcompany.com (accessed 10 April 2017).
2. Malcolm, H. (2015). 'How Nike Plans to Turn Women's Fitness into an $11 Billion Empire'. [online] *USA Today*. Available at: usatoday.com (accessed 10 April 2017).
3. Cramphorn, op. cit.

CHAPTER 6

1. Mamamia (2015). 'Tony Abbott as Minister for Women: A Report Card'. [online] *Mamamia*. Available at: mamamia.com.au (accessed 10 April 2017).

2. Flood, A. (2016). 'Girl's drive to find 1000 "black girl books" hits target with outpouring of donations'. [online] *The Guardian*. Available at: theguardian.com (accessed 10 April 2017).
3. Wellington City Council (2014). *Light Shed on Kate Sheppard*. [online] Available at: wellington.govt.nz (accessed 10 April 2017).
4. Staufenberg, J. (2016). 'London Pride: Gay and trans replace green man on traffic pedestrian crossings for festival'. [online] *Independent*. Available at: independent.co.uk (accessed 10 April 2017).
5. Gray, Y. (2017). 'Female light signals to go up at pedestrian crossing as Committee for Melbourne tackles "unconcious bias"'. [online] *ABC News*. Available at: abc.net.au (accessed 10 April 2017).
6. *Herald Sun* (2017). 'State Government Minister Calls for More Female Statutes as Gender Equality Measure'. [online] *Herald Sun*. Available at: heraldsun.com.au (accessed 10 April 2017).
7. *The Drum* (2017). 'Spike in Tropfest finalists after filmmakers' names were removed from the submissions'. [video]. Available at: the drum.com.au (accessed 10 April 2017).
8. *AdNews* (2016). 'Where's the money going? Exclusive ad spend trends report'. [online] *AdNews*. Available at: adnews.com.au (accessed 10 April 2017).
9. TAC (2016). 'Introducing Graham: the one person designed to survive roads'. [online] TAC. Available at: tac.vic.gov.au (accessed 10 April 2017).

CHAPTER 7

1. The World Bank, (2015). 'Population, female (% of total)'. [online] Available at: data.worldbank.org (Accessed 13 June 2017)

CHAPTER 8

1. Etcoff, N., Orbach, S., Scott, J. & D'Agostino, H. (2004). *The Real Truth About Beauty: A Global Report*. [online] Amsterdam: The Club of Amsterdam. Available at: clubofamsterdam.com (accessed 10 April 2017).
2. Neff, J. (2014.) 'Ten Years In, Dove's "Real Beauty" Seems to Be Aging Well'. [online] *Advertising Age*. Available at: adage.com (accessed 10 April 2017).
3. Zhang, M. (2013). 'Dove Speaks Out Against Retouching by Releasing Anti-Photoshop Action'. [online] *Petapixel*. Available at: petapixel.com (accessed 10 April 2017).
4. Dove Self-esteem Project (2015). *Dove Self-esteem Project*. [online]. Available at: selfesteem.mydove.com.au (accessed 10 April 2017).
5. Piaget, J. & Cook, M. (1952). *The Origins of Intelligence in Children*. New York, NY: International University Press.

CONCLUSION

1. Ponce De Leon, C. (2015). 'That's the Way It Is: A History of Television News in America'. [online] University of Chicago Press Books. Available at: press.uchicago.edu (accessed 10 April 2017).
2. Courtney, P. (2016). 'Carrots: Girl Power'. [online] *ABC Landline*. Available at: abc.net.au (accessed 10 April 2017).

IMAGE CREDITS

pp. 52: eye testing and eye exam chart © robertlamphoto / Shutterstock

pp. 56–57: Business women © Nevena Radonja / Shutterstock

pp. 58, 61: furniture © Room27 / Shutterstock

pp. 64: Credit card terminal isolated on white on right side of the picture © Alex Kuzhak / Shutterstock

pp. 65: Bill or receipt over light blue background © Route66 / Shutterstock

pp. 68, 71: collection of various cardboard boxes on white background © Picsfive/Shutterstock

pp. 71, 72: Opened cardboard package, isolated, white background © Karramba Production / Shutterstock

pp. 76: Perfume bottle isolated on white background © Hekla / Shutterstock

pp. 77: Men perfume isolated on a white background © Ivan Kurmyshov / Shutterstock

pp. 79: White smartphone mockup © Alexey Boldin / Shutterstock

pp. 85: Collection of crowns / vintage illustration from Meyers Konversations-Lexikon 1897 © Hein Nouwens / Shutterstock

pp. 86: Clever young woman in spectacles with long blond hair © sanneberg / Shutterstock

pp. 87: Portrait of a smart serious young man standing against building. Long blond hair © Uber Images / Shutterstock

pp. 91: White smartphone mockup © Alexey Boldin / Shutterstock; Face of an young black beauty in black and white © And-One / Shutterstock

pp. 92, 94: The isolated image of three green plastic toy soldiers © Panayu Chairatananond / Shutterstock

pp. 96: 2000s UK Dove Magazine Advert © The Advertising Archives / Alamy Stock Photo

pp. 101: 1950s USA Chase and Sanborn Magazine Advert © The Advertising Archives / Alamy Stock Photo